AF728866

COFFEE SHOP

AT HOME

COFFEE SHOP

AT HOME

The Ultimate Guide to Making
Your Favorite Coffee Drinks

Katerina Diaz

PHOTOGRAPHS BY DOAA ELKADY
ILLUSTRATIONS BY ELIZABETH HART

CLARKSON POTTER/PUBLISHERS
New York

CONTENTS

To my grandma Wella,
who showed me life's
sweetest moments are best
enjoyed over coffee.

INTRODUCTION

My philosophy is this: Life is too short to drink mediocre coffee.

Many of us drink coffee at least once a day, and I believe every coffee-drinking experience should be a positive one. Coffee is a source of joy for me each morning, and something I look forward to when I go to sleep at night. I want this book to be like a lighthouse for you, guiding you toward the best possible at-home coffee experience. Because at the end of the day, no one cares more about your coffee experience than you do (well, except for me, but I can't be there to make your coffee every day).

I spent too many years of my life overpaying for and drinking mediocre brews because I lacked the confidence to learn how to make a great cup at home. When I finally committed to practicing and learned how simple at-home coffee can be, I wished I had started sooner. The fact that you're reading this right now tells me you too want to improve your coffee skills. I am here to help.

In August 2021, I began my at-home coffee journey. I started posting recipes and coffee education content on my website and social channels because I wanted to share the techniques I was learning and the knowledge I was acquiring with others. Whenever I was asked a question I didn't know the answer to, I researched or practiced techniques to better assist others with their at-home coffee. Five years and hundreds of thousands of coffee fans later, I've distilled all my knowledge and coffee expertise into this book.

With *Coffee Shop at Home*, I want to help you increase your own coffee knowledge, learn how to re-create all your favorite coffee-shop drinks at home, fall even more in love with coffee, and become more confident in your coffee-making abilities, no matter what type of drinks you enjoy most. This book will set you up for success whether you're crafting a single cup for yourself or you are the barista when hosting friends and family.

My hope is that through the information and recipes within these pages, you'll become an equipped at-home barista who prefers making coffee at home rather than buying from a shop, and who has an infinite number of drink recipes in your toolbelt. And along the way, I hope you'll embrace the imperfect moments, too. Early in my coffee journey, I accidentally melted a Torani vanilla bottle by leaving it too close to my air fryer, and it curved into a swan neck-shaped bottle. Three years later I still refill that wonderfully wonky bottle, now named Veronica. She's my daily reminder that learning to make great coffee is a process, and that the joy is found not just in the perfect cup, but in the imperfect, memorable moments you collect along the way.

The first part of this book will walk you through the fundamentals of coffee. I discuss topics like coffee origins, roast levels, flavor notes, processing methods, and grind size and how all of these affect how each cup of coffee tastes. Understanding the characteristics of various coffees will allow you to make coffees with the qualities you enjoy most. This section also covers the different at-home brewing methods so you can choose the best ones for your lifestyle and budget.

The second part of the book dives into recipes that include coffeehouse-level mochas, lattes, shaken espressos, Americanos, iced coffees, cold brews, and frappes. In addition to coffee drinks, there are also affogatos, chais, and matchas. This book will allow you to whip up all of your coffee-shop favorites anytime you want them, and for a fraction of the price. And yes, I mean making a Pumpkin Cream Cold Brew in the middle of April if that is what your heart desires.

Throughout my college years and early adult life, I—like many of you, I'm sure—bought an iced coffee every day before school or work. I tried making my own drinks at home to save money (that $3.25 per day was pretty painful for a college student), but no matter what I did, I always ended up pouring the coffee down the drain. I felt so reliant on coffee shops to give me a good coffee every day that I'd ignore the fact that some days they'd forget the sweetener or wouldn't add enough cream, or the topping was missing, or the coffee tasted like burnt computer cables. Week after week, I'd reload my card and turn a blind eye to my dwindling bank account.

But one day, I decided to add up my monthly coffee charges, and I was utterly blown away when I saw that the total was in the $300 range. I'd known I was spending a lot, but hot diggity, that was a significant chunk of my paycheck! Yet when I thought of the alternative—subpar coffee made at home—I was able to justify to myself that it was okay to spend that much on coffee as long as I was enjoying it.

As the months went by, I switched from iced coffee to lattes, which literally doubled the price I was paying each day. The price increase hurt, and I couldn't help but notice more and more that my coffee was disappointing. And now that I was paying more, I found myself agitated anytime the topping was missing, or the cold foam was nonexistent, or the color was completely wrong. But I felt like a nuisance always asking the baristas to fix my drinks, so sometimes I just accepted the bad coffee.

Finally, I realized something: no one else cared about my coffee experience as much as I did, so why did I constantly put the responsibility in other people's hands? If I knew exactly how I wanted my coffee to taste (and look), why wasn't I making it myself?

So I decided to make it my mission to learn how to make my coffee at home, exactly how I wanted it.

I researched various coffee roasts. I learned about the different brewing methods, like pour-over versus cold brew versus espresso, and I learned how to make different drinks with those methods. For example, to make a simple iced latte, you start by making espresso (using an espresso machine, Moka pot, or AeroPress or other method), then combine the espresso with milk and ice. You can easily create any latte you want by adding a flavored syrup. For an Iced Blueberry Vanilla Latte (page 124), just add my Blueberry Vanilla Syrup. To make a hot mocha, you want chocolate sauce, espresso, and steamed milk. You can add cinnamon and cayenne for a Mexican Mocha vibe (page 88) or swap the steamed milk for cold milk and ice to create an iced version.

I learned how iced coffee and cold brews are made with different brewing methods. Iced coffee is brewed hot and then chilled, while cold brew is brewed cold (hence the name), and although they can be served similarly—add a syrup or flavored creamer or cold foam as you like—they taste drastically different. The same also goes for a coffee-pot cup of coffee and a hot Americano. The two may look similar and seem to just be a cup of coffee, but they are wildly different in taste, acidity, body, and so forth because of their different brewing methods.

For frappes or blended coffee drinks, I learned that using instant coffee powder rather than liquid coffee is best for giving you that bold coffee flavor without watering them down.

I discovered that you can create different espresso drinks by changing the "base" of the drink (e.g., water, milk, or half-and-half) or adjusting the ratio of espresso to milk (as in a latte versus a macchiato) to make a more- or less-coffee-forward beverage.

I quickly realized that making coffee at home was much more enjoyable than buying it every day, and I discovered how much fun it was to create different flavor combos to make any coffee beverage my mind could imagine! Oftentimes I would crave a holiday drink like gingerbread, eggnog, peppermint mocha, or pumpkin spice coffee but my local coffee shops didn't have these seasonal favorites. Making my own versions meant that I could enjoy them any time of year. It's important to note, I never want to shame anyone for buying coffee if it's something that brings them joy. It used to bring me joy, until one day it didn't anymore.

This book is for anyone who is tired of overpaying for mediocre coffee, and wants to learn how to make all their coffee-shop favorites at home for much cheaper.

I want to help you get to the point where your own creations are unmatched, and no coffee shop can offer you a better cup of Joe than the one you make yourself. Why? Because friends don't let friends drink mediocre coffee. You can learn to make all your go-to coffee-shop drinks without any fancy equipment or barista training, and you can transform your home into your own coffee shop—you just need this book.

WHY MAKE COFFEE AT HOME?

I used to view at-home coffee as an inferior option: it didn't taste great, but it was cost-effective, so you just dealt with it. My brain always went to Keurig coffee or coffee-pot coffee with a flavored creamer, and I never realized it could be so much more than that. Making coffee at home means you can create a drink perfectly curated to your preferences every single day. It's a way to control your finances and reduce mindless spending. It allows you to make more eco-friendly and health-conscious choices, and at the end of the day, it is a very rewarding practice.

AT HOME COFFEE IS . . .

Endlessly customizable: Sure, you can choose a different milk option or a different syrup flavor at a coffee shop, but at home you can customize your drink exactly the way you want it. You choose the beans to use, the amount of creamer and the milk that you like, the syrup you prefer—you control it all! At-home coffee makes the coffee experience so personal. You are your own barista, and the combinations you can create are limitless!

Less expensive: When you make coffee at home, it is definitely cheaper, even if you use expensive beans or buy a fancy machine. And think about the money you save on tips and taxes, the savings in gas you would otherwise spend on driving to the coffee shop, and the time sitting in the drive-thru line. The savings add up exponentially, especially if you normally order multiple drinks a day. (See page 15 for more!)

SUSTAINABILITY AND ETHICAL CHOICES

At-home coffee allows for more sustainable and ethical coffee choices, such as:

- **Choosing reusable cups, lids, straws, and coffee sleeves instead of single-use options.** Swapping single-use items for reusable ones is one of the easiest and most impactful steps you can take toward a more sustainable coffee routine. Just think about how many paper and plastic cups are used and tossed every single day at coffee shops, most of which are not recycled. At home, you can opt for reusable glassware and mugs instead of disposable plastic. A fun tip: check your local thrift store for Mason jars, coffee mugs, or even cute tumblers.

- **Buying coffee from roasters that use biodegradable packaging.** You'll notice many of the coffee bags at grocery stores are made of plastic. Recently I've seen a shift, with coffee brands, especially smaller coffee roasters, switching to biodegradable bags and packaging. When shopping for beans, consider supporting companies that prioritize eco-friendly packaging.

- **Buying coffee from roasters that ensure their farmer partners and laborers are fairly compensated.** One of the biggest benefits of making coffee at home is that it gives you more control over where your beans come from. Buying from roasters who prioritize ethical sourcing and fair compensation for their farmers helps support a more humane and ethical coffee system. Many of these roasters work directly with smaller farms, compensate accordingly, and invest in long-term partnerships to support both the environment and the well-being of the community. When you brew at home with intentionally sourced coffee, you're contributing to a more just and sustainable coffee industry (and you'll be drinking great coffee too!).

- **Buying coffee from roasters that ensure the coffee is grown and processed using environmentally friendly practices.** When you are brewing your own coffee, you have the opportunity to choose beans that align with your values, starting with how they're grown. Many specialty roasters source coffee that's been grown and processed using environmentally responsible practices, including organic farming, water conservation, and reduced pesticide use. These practices help preserve biodiversity and soil health and also support long-term sustainability for farming communities. Look for local roasters and coffee shops that prioritize environmentally friendly practices. If you're not sure, check their websites, or ask a barista.

- **Reusing coffee grounds for composting, deodorizing your fridge, or mixing with soil for fertilizing.** One of the simplest ways to make your at-home coffee routine more sustainable is reusing your coffee grounds. Coffee grounds are rich in nitrogen, making them a great addition to compost piles or soil blends, and they're great for absorbing undesirable smells. Instead of tossing them in the trash, compost them to enrich your garden soil, sprinkle them into the soil in potted plants as a natural fertilizer, or even save them to help neutralize odors in your fridge or freezer. Reusing the grounds is a low-effort way to extend the life of something you'd normally throw out, all while giving back to the earth—and your home.

More mindful: Making coffee at home can be a mindful practice. You're more cognizant of what exactly is going into your cup as well as of how much money goes into creating your drink. As someone with a nutrition background, I try my best to be aware of my daily sugar intake. I feel my best when I don't overdo it on sugar, and making my own coffee allows me to adjust the sweetness to my preference and focus on a healthy balance.

Better for the environment: At home, you can choose reusable cups, lids, straws, and coffee sleeves. And many coffee roasters offer biodegradable packaging these days. You can also select coffee brands that support local farmers and that grow their coffee sustainably. Small changes like these make a real impact on the environment. (See page 13 for more on this too!)

Personally rewarding: Making coffee at home can be a fun and rewarding process. Before you know it, it will become a hobby that you look forward to knowing more about and fine-tuning your skills. Take steaming milk, for example. You can start by learning to steam milk perfectly for hot lattes, and then you can take that skill further by practicing your latte art and creating different shapes. We've probably all dumped disappointing coffee down the drain at one point in our lives, but I hope this book encourages you to view at-home coffee as an enjoyable learning process.

IS AT-HOME COFFEE REALLY CHEAPER?

The short answer is, Yes. But I want to dive deeper into this point because, for many of you, that is the main reason you're reading this book right now.

I am an incredibly frugal person. When I was a kid, my parents would give me and my sister $5.00 each to spend on snacks at the gas station. My sister would come home with one $4.99 family-size bag of chips, and I'd come home with twenty different $0.25 pieces of candy. I loved feeling like I got the biggest bang for my buck, and now, as an adult, I still try to be conscious of how I spend my money.

I used to feel so much guilt when reloading my Starbucks card and swiping it every day, but I felt like I didn't have any other choice. I didn't know how to make great-tasting coffee at home, so I continued to justify the amount I spent on my daily coffee shop purchases to myself.

One day, I sat down to see exactly how much money I was spending each month on coffee, and I couldn't believe the total.

I decided I had to find a way to start making coffee

at home, and I began doing the math for various machines. Then I calculated the cost of the machine, the coffee, and the syrup and milk and compared that to my monthly coffee-shop expenses.

I learned that even if I bought a $600 espresso machine, I would still spend less in a year than if I continued buying coffee every day. Let me break it down for you:

- $600 machine divided by 365 days = $1.64/day
- $20 for 20 bags of coffee beans (to make a double shot of espresso every day for a year, I'd need twenty 12-ounce bags) = $400/year, or $1.09/day
- $7 for 8 bottles of syrup (I use a tablespoon of syrup in my coffee every day, so I'd need about 8 bottles of syrup for a year) = $56/year, or $0.15/day
- $2.16 for 23 gallons of milk (for an 8-ounce latte every day, I'd need a total of 23 gallons of milk) = $50/year, or $0.14/day

DAILY TOTAL: $3.02
($1.64 + $1.09 + $0.15 + $0.14)

WEEKLY TOTAL: $21.14
($3.02 X 7 days)

YEARLY TOTAL: $1,099
($21.14 X 52 weeks)

So, for one year of making coffee at home using a $600 espresso machine, the total price comes out to $1,099. But if I continued making coffee at home for a second year, I wouldn't need to factor in the machine cost, so my yearly expenses would be: $502.32 ($1.09 + $0.15 + $0.14 per day for 52 weeks).

But if I bought a double-shot latte every day from a coffee shop, my daily total would be: $6.43. And that could be more if I substituted the flavor of syrup or asked for a different milk. So, my weekly total expenses would be $45.01, and the total for a year would be $2,341.

AT-HOME COFFEE VERSUS COFFEE SHOP COFFEE

(Based on a double-shot latte every day)

	DAILY	WEEKLY	MONTHLY	YEARLY
AT HOME	$3.02	$21.14	$82 to $94	$1,099
COFFEE SHOP	$6.43	$45.01	$174 to $199	$2,341
DIFFERENCE	*$3.41*	*$23.87*	*$92 TO $105*	*$1,242*

Now, I don't know about you, but if there's a way to save $1,200 a year, I am all about it! And if you have a spouse, a partner, a roommate, or other family members, the savings would be $3,000 or more per year. It is much more cost-effective to make coffee at home, even with a $600 espresso machine in the equation—and your savings would be exponentially greater if using a more affordable coffee brewer like a Moka pot, French press, AeroPress, or a pour-over.

Another factor to consider is a rise in coffee prices. This could be because of tariffs, climate change, global demand, minimum-wage increases, or even supply-chain disruptions. Making coffee at home allows you to select the beans, roasters, and brewing methods that best suit your budget. Because coffee shops will undoubtedly increase their prices year after year, making coffee at home remains the more cost-effective option. Making your own syrups and sauces rather than buying them is another way to cut down on costs.

MY AT-HOME COFFEE JOURNEY

After we'd realized how much money we could save by making our coffee at home,

the first thing my husband and I did was buy an inexpensive espresso machine. I knew I wanted to make lattes every day, so I bought a $40 machine and a bag of Starbucks espresso-roast coffee, since I loved Starbucks' espresso. But the first latte I made tasted absolutely horrible. I dumped it down the drain and found myself in the coffee shop drive-thru line again.

I tried a few more times and had the same awful experience each time. So we returned the machine and somehow talked ourselves into buying a much more expensive espresso machine, a Breville Barista Express. It was the biggest purchase we had ever made, but we both committed to learning how to use the machine.

The very first extraction tasted quite good, and significantly better than the espresso from the $40 machine. Then the first vanilla latte we made tasted a lot like the one at Starbucks, and we were jazzed!

I researched more ways to improve our espresso-machine experience, and I learned there are so many variables that play a role in the overall extraction:

- You can use any coffee beans you like in an espresso machine; you don't have to use beans that that are labeled "espresso." And while some roasters label the coffee "espresso beans" because they roast the beans with the intent for them to be brewed as espresso, you can use them however you'd like. In fact, you can use any beans for any brewing method you prefer.
- Good-quality beans make a difference, as does their freshness. Opting for roast-to-order beans rather than buying roasted beans lets you know exactly how fresh the coffee is so you can produce the best tasting extractions.
- Freshly ground beans will give you the best-tasting espresso. Grinding the beans right before each extraction is well worth the effort, no matter which brewing method or machine you're using.
- Grinding your beans finer will result in increasing the pressure during espresso extraction; grinding them coarser, in turn, will reduce the pressure during extraction.
- It's important to weigh the beans and time the extraction for the most consistent espresso extractions.

I slowly switched from using all Starbucks products and started buying coffee from other brands or from local coffee shops. Along the way, I noticed a drastic difference in how much better my drinks started tasting, and I discovered my coffee was so much more delicious than I'd imagined. I started detecting flavor notes in my coffee that I'd never noticed before, and I began to become more aware of acidity and bitterness in some coffees. I felt like my whole world opened up as I learned how to make good coffee at home.

I realized that there was so much more to at-home coffee than I had thought, and not only did I want to learn more for myself, I wanted to share everything that I was learning with others. So I started posting a few coffee recipes to my Instagram account. I received some questions that I knew the answers to, and others I had no idea how to answer. But anytime I wasn't sure, I'd do the research so I could respond to them. Before I knew it, people were coming to me with all their coffee questions and recipe requests, and now my entire career is centered around teaching others how to make amazing coffee at home! With this book, I want to provide you with all the tools you need to be successful with your own at-home coffee so you don't have to waste your time or money trying to find the best coffee-making processes and recipes. I want to help you start saving money now and making all of your own favorite drinks *today*!

COFFEE

FUNDAMENTALS

LET'S TALK COFFEE

BASIC TERMINOLOGY AND FINDING YOUR PERSONAL PREFERENCES

One of the things I love about coffee is that there's always something new to discover. Whether it's a different brewing method, an unfamiliar origin, or a surprising flavor note, every cup offers a chance to learn and experience something unique. The more you explore, the more your coffee knowledge and coffee vocabulary will grow. What once tasted "sour" to you might later be better described as "bright," "fruity," or "acidic." It's all part of the journey.

In this section, I explore some of the language used to describe different coffees, such as "flavor notes," "body," "acidity," and "aftertaste." These are all terms used in the coffee space that can help anyone talk about what they like or don't like in a cup of coffee. You don't always need to get it "right," learning these terms is just a great way to start noticing what stands out to you in any coffee.

Maybe you prefer coffee that is smooth and mild. Maybe you love a bold, dark roast. You might want to say, "This coffee tastes rich and chocolatey," or "I like this one because it's not too bitter." That's all part of developing your palate and your confidence.

A good place to start is by paying attention to the flavor descriptions on the coffee bags or roasters' websites. If you know you like chocolate or caramel, look for a coffee that mentions those flavor notes and see if you can pick them out as you're tasting the coffee. Then try a coffee with completely different flavor notes, like one with berry or citrus notes, and compare the two.

You could also explore how different brewing methods or roast levels affect the taste. The goal here is to help you become more comfortable identifying what you enjoy and why, so you can not only drink great coffee, but you can talk about it too. This chapter will give you the vocabulary, knowledge, and confidence to do just that.

THE COFFEE DICTIONARY

I've put together this mini coffee dictionary of coffee-related vocabulary to help you grow in your coffee knowledge and also help you learn to "speak coffee." Use these words and definitions as a jumping-off point in your coffee conversations and to guide your coffee drinking and purchasing.

ACIDITY: Refers to a flavor element in coffee often perceived as bright, tangy, or sharp on the tongue. Acidity in coffee doesn't mean sour: it's the brightness or liveliness of the flavor and can range from low to high. A coffee's origin, roast level, and brewing method can all play a role in its acidity.

AFTERTASTE: The lingering flavors a coffee leaves in your mouth after you swallow. Some coffees may have a long, pleasant aftertaste, while others may be harsh and bitter or fade quickly.

AROMA: The fragrance or smell of a coffee. You may experience a coffee's aroma both before and after it's roasted, before and after grinding the beans, during the brewing process, and once it is poured into a cup or carafe.

BODY: The texture and mouthfeel of a coffee on your tongue. As with milk, where skim milk (light body) has a thinner texture and mouthfeel than whole milk (full body), light-body coffees taste lighter, thinner, and more delicate on the tongue whereas full body coffees tend to leave a thicker, almost creamy mouthfeel. Roast level and brewing method can both affect a coffee's body.

CAFFEINE: A naturally occurring stimulant found in coffee beans, tea leaves, and cacao pods that can help you feel more awake, alert, and focused.

EXTRACTION: Refers to the process of pulling flavor and aroma out of coffee grounds using hot (or cold) water. As the water flows through the grounds, it dissolves the compounds that give coffee its taste and smell. Those dissolved flavors are what make up the delicious brew you sip from your cup.

FLAVOR NOTES: The inherent flavors and aromas of coffee beans. Not to be confused with flavored coffee, these notes occur naturally in coffee beans; flavored coffees have flavorings that are added to the beans. Like wine, different coffees can have distinct and complex flavor notes. (See page 28 for more.)

ORIGIN: Refers to the regions and countries where coffee beans are grown and sourced from (e.g., Ethiopia, Colombia, and Brazil). Different coffees have distinct flavor profiles and characteristics because of varying soil, altitude, and climate of these regions.

PROCESSING: Processing is the method used to remove the seeds from coffee cherries so they are ready for roasting. Each process affects the way the coffee bean tastes.

- **Natural-Process (Dry-Process):** For this method, the whole coffee cherries are dried in the sun. During drying, the coffee cherries ferment, developing more sweetness and flavor. Once dried, the pulp and skin are removed from the seed, resulting in a sweet, juicy, syrupy coffee when brewed.

- **Washed-Process:** Here the seeds are removed from the coffee cherry, then washed to remove any skin, pulp, or mucilage and dried in the sun. This process results in a cleaner, brighter, more acidic coffee.

- **Honey-Process (Pulped Natural-Process):** This method combines components of the natural-processed and washed-processed techniques, whereby the coffee seed is removed from the coffee cherry but the mucilage is left on it throughout the drying process. This method results in a balanced coffee that is sweet but also has pronounced acidity.

- **Wet-Hulled Process (Semi-Washed Processed):** Most commonly practiced in Indonesia, this is a method where the parchment layer (the natural, protective layer of cellulose around the coffee seed) is removed before they are fully dry. The seeds are removed from the coffee cherries, but some of the mucilage is left on them. The seeds are placed in a fermentation tank overnight and then dried for just a short time before the parchment layer is removed and the seeds are fully dried. This process results in a chocolatey, more savory, and nuttier-tasting coffee.

ROAST LEVEL: The degree to which green coffee beans are roasted to achieve the desired color, flavor, and aroma.

- **Light Roast:** Lighter brown in color than other roasts, these beans preserve much of their flavor; they are the highest in acidity. (Flavor notes may include bright, acidic, and, often, fruity.)

- **Medium Roast:** These medium-brown beans have less of their natural flavor and more of a roasted flavor; they also have less acidity than light roast coffees. (Flavor notes may include balanced, smooth, and slightly sweet.)

- **Dark Roast:** These beans are dark brown, shiny, and oily, with a smokier roasted flavor and the lowest acidity of all the roast levels. (Flavor notes may include bold, smoky, and chocolatey.)

COFFEE ROASTS

Roast level is the most commonly mentioned characteristic when talking about coffee beans. The term refers to how long the beans were roasted for and at what temperature. A coffee roaster is essentially an oven for coffee beans that has a rotating drum or other components to ensure even roasting. After processing, the coffee beans are light green. They are then roasted until they are aromatic and darker in color, or, as Michael Scott from *The Office* would say, "Boom, roasted." Then the beans are transferred to a cooling tray and the beans are cooled with water or air to stop the roasting process. Each level has its own characteristics, and it's helpful to try out the various roast options to find your personal preference.

LIGHT ROAST

Coffee beans (or grounds) labeled "light roast" have been roasted for less time and at a lower temperature than medium or dark-roast coffee. These beans are a lighter brown than the other roasts. Light-roast coffee typically has a brighter or more acidic taste because the shorter time and lower temperature preserve a lot of the beans' natural acids. Acidity or brightness in coffee is not necessarily a bad thing, but some people may prefer a darker roast with less acidity. Light-roast coffees taste less bitter than darker roasts and may have less body or thickness when brewed. Because light-roast coffee is subjected to less heat, the beans retain much of their original aroma and flavor. Some coffee shops label their lighter-roast coffees "blonde roast."

MEDIUM ROAST

Medium-roast coffee beans are roasted at a higher temperature and for a longer period of time than light-roast coffee beans. They're a medium-brown color and less acidic than lighter roasts; the beans have a well-rounded flavor profile with a good balance of acidity, sweetness, and body. Since medium-roast coffee beans are roasted for a longer time than light-roast beans, they lose more of their natural flavor and aroma, but the longer roasting makes them more balanced and roasty in flavor.

DARK ROAST

Dark-roast coffees are dark brown (almost black) and have an oily or shiny appearance because of the higher temperatures and longer roast times. Darker roasts go through the biggest chemical changes, resulting in a larger loss of their natural flavors and aroma. Much of the flavors you taste in a dark roast, such as increased bitterness and texture or body, are the result of the roasting process itself. The longer roasting time brings out more of the beans' savory notes, and you'll often taste bold, smoky, chocolate, or licorice flavors. Dark-roast coffee tends to be lower in acidity than light or medium roasts.

When it comes to selecting the best coffee roast, there are no wrong answers: it all boils down to what you like best. And your selection may also change depending on the brewing method you're using. For example, you may find you enjoy a lighter roast for a pour-over coffee, but you prefer a medium roast for a cold brew. I recommend asking a barista at your favorite coffee shop which beans and roast they use to make your coffee so you can start learning which roast(s) you gravitate toward. Many shops have various drip-coffee options, so you can order cups of coffee with different roast levels to see which you prefer.

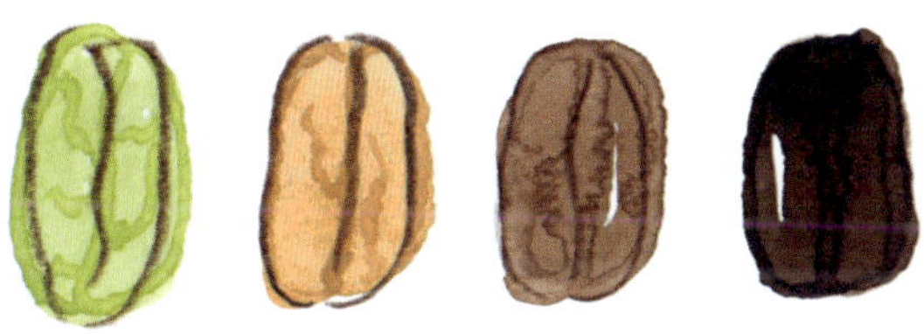

FLAVOR NOTES

In addition to the roast level, different coffees have different flavor notes: think chocolatey, fruity, citrus, caramel, nutty, and/or smoky. The region the coffee is from and the processing method used also affect the coffees' flavor notes. Just as every wine has its own unique aromas and flavor profiles, so does coffee.

Common flavor notes you'll find in coffee:

- **Fruity:** blueberry, blackberry, cherry, apple, or orange
- **Sweet:** honey, brown sugar, maple syrup, caramel, or molasses
- **Spice:** cloves, cinnamon, nutmeg, anise, or pepper
- **Nutty:** peanuts, almonds, hazelnuts, or even cocoa and chocolate
- **Floral:** chamomile, rose, or jasmine

You don't need to be a flavor note expert to make great coffee at home, but having a basic understanding of the notes and which you prefer makes it easier to select beans you'll enjoy most.

A great way to practice identifying flavor notes is to read coffee bag labels and then find these notes in your cup of coffee. Before brewing the coffee, give the bag of beans a deep sniff and try to identify some of those flavor notes. Grind the beans, and sniff the coffee again. You may notice even more of the flavor notes. Brew the coffee, stir, and sniff once more, trying to identify more flavor notes. Lastly, scoop up a spoonful of coffee and slurp it, paying attention to all the flavors. Try this technique with different coffees and see if you can identify the various aromas.

Another way to improve this skill is to attend a coffee-tasting class. Many coffee shops host events like these where they explain the different flavor notes of various coffees. Afterward, you can have your own tasting class at home, brewing different coffees using the same brewing method and tasting each one to see which you like most. This will help you identify the flavor notes you prefer, so you can try new brands with those notes.

Establish which coffee characteristics you enjoy most, and always keep an open mind when it comes to discovering new roast levels, origins, or flavor notes.

Credit: Specialty Coffee Association, World Coffee Research, and UC Davis Coffee Center

SCA

Coffee Taster's Flavor Wheel

Specialty Coffee Association

WORLD COFFEE RESEARCH

UC DAVIS COFFEE CENTER

COFFEE TASTER'S FLAVOR WHEEL CREATED USING THE SENSORY LEXICON DEVELOPED BY WORLD COFFEE RESEARCH

© 2016 SCA AND WCR

V.2

COFFEE CHARACTERISTICS BY REGION

Here are the most common characteristics you can expect to find in coffees from the following continents and countries.

REGION / CONTINENT	GENERAL CHARACTERISTICS	NOTABLE COUNTRIES AND FLAVOR PROFILES
Africa	Medium to high acidity Floral, citrus, berry notes; bright, fragrant, often sweet	**Ethiopia:** Fruity, smooth, syrupy mouthfeel, sometimes light body **Kenya:** Sweet, slightly tart, mellow, well-balanced **Tanzania:** Bright, wine-like, strong acidity
Asia & Oceania	Low acidity Spicy, earthy, dark chocolate notes	**Indonesia (Sumatra):** Bold, full-bodied, earthy; often wet-hulled processed because of the climate **Malaysia:** Fruity, nutty, clean, strong
South America	Low to medium acidity Chocolate and caramel notes; smooth, crisp, clean; bright aftertaste	**Brazil:** Low acidity, caramely, chocolatey, nutty; often espresso roasts **Colombia:** Fruity, sweet, candy-like; full body; well-balanced with slight acidity **Peru:** Smooth, mellow, nutty-sweet; mild acidity; light to medium body
Central America	Medium to high acidity Nutty and fruity	**Costa Rica:** Earthy, herbal, citrusy; bright acidity; subtly sweet with tropical/stone fruit **El Salvador:** Medium to full body; sweet, bright, clean; citrusy or chocolatey; some floral varietals **Guatemala:** Rich, flavorful, slightly acidic, sometimes smoky **Honduras:** Sweet, fruity, balanced, nutty **Nicaragua:** Extremely tart, sometimes chocolatey **Panama:** Well-balanced, sweet, fruity, citrusy; known for the Geisha varietal

CAFFEINE IN COFFEE

We all process caffeine differently, so understanding your caffeine tolerance and how caffeine affects your body is important. For some, a cup of coffee comes before a restorative nap. For others, it causes jitters and heart palpitations. I've learned I cannot drink any form of caffeine after 3 p.m. if I want to fall asleep at a normal hour. Here I want to touch on a few ways you can be more mindful of caffeine and how you can choose the best coffee options for you.

NOT ALL COFFEE HAS EQUAL CAFFEINE LEVELS

Both the coffee beans and the brewing method you use affect the amount of caffeine in your cup. While it's true that an 8-ounce serving of cold brew typically contains more caffeine than an 8-ounce pour-over coffee, it's difficult to make definitive claims about caffeine levels. In general, cold brew and espresso tend to have higher amounts of caffeine than coffee made with another method. Of course, opting for a latte with three or four shots of espresso will certainly give you a caffeine jolt. And many other variables can determine caffeine content. Factors including grind size, extraction time, and coffee-to-water ratio all play a role. It's also worth mentioning that most caffeine measurements are estimates, as these variables can differ. Even two brands of cold brew can have different caffeine levels due to variations in beans, ratios, and brew times. Understanding that caffeine levels can vary significantly from cup to cup is important.

WHEN IN DOUBT, CHOOSE DECAF

I think decaf coffee gets a bad rap. I always hear people say decaf is pointless since there's no caffeine in it, but I disagree. First, decaf coffee still has some caffeine, although significantly less than regular coffee. Usually a cup of regular coffee has around 95 mg of caffeine, and a cup of decaf has 2 to 3 mg. Second, I wholeheartedly believe that there is room for decaf in a whole slew of circumstances. It's a great option for new moms, pregnant women, or anyone needing to limit their caffeine. I frequently opt for decaf as my second coffee of the day, and it's phenomenal for late-night coffee desserts, like my Salted Cookie Butter Affogato (page 217).

If you are a decaf coffee drinker, you can still make every recipe in this book! Simply use decaf coffee beans or grounds (or a decaf coffee product).

READ THE LABEL

Many bags of coffee don't list caffeine amounts, but some store-bought coffees do include this on the nutrition label. If you are curious about the amount of caffeine in a particular coffee, check the serving size on the nutrition label. To ensure you are consuming the same amount of caffeine listed on the label, use a food scale or a Mason jar with measurements to measure the amount of coffee. Many brands, though, do not disclose the amount of caffeine on the nutrition label, so you may need to call the customer service number or check the brand's website. It's always a good idea to be aware of how much caffeine you are consuming, whether you experience noticeable caffeine side effects or not.

MUSHROOM COFFEE

I am not the biggest mushroom coffee fan; in fact, I wouldn't call myself a fan at all, but I do think it's worth mentioning it. Mushroom coffee is a product that combines medicinal mushrooms (like chaga, lion's mane, and reishi) and ground coffee for a lower-caffeine, less acidic coffee option. I won't get into whether mushroom coffee can in fact improve overall health or not, but it is a lower-caffeine alternative that you may want to check out.

I hope this section helped you better understand coffee and gave you the confidence to lead the coffee conversation during a coffee date with a friend or at a family gathering. Next comes the fun part: shopping!

SHOPPING FOR COFFEE

BUYING AND STORING GUIDE

Now that we've established how to talk about coffee and many of its characteristics, it's time to buy some. This can be a very personal experience because it all comes down to what you like most. What roast level, flavor notes, processing, and brewing methods do you prefer? To narrow down the options, I recommend asking yourself a few questions before buying a bag (or container, or bottle, or box, or sleeve) of coffee.

QUESTION 1: WHAT TYPE OF COFFEE DRINKS DO I USUALLY BUY FROM COFFEE SHOPS?

- Espresso drinks like lattes, mochas, shaken espressos, macchiatos, flat whites, etc.
- Cold brew
- Drip coffee
- Iced coffee
- Frappes

The type of coffee beverages you like to drink and order will determine which coffees you should buy.

QUESTION 2: WHAT ROAST DO I LIKE BEST?

- Think light (aka blonde) roast, medium roast, or dark roast. (See page 26 for more information.)
- Do you prefer specific roasts based on the brewing method? For example, blonde-roast espresso, medium-roast drip coffee, dark-roast espresso.

Cold brews and iced coffees are typically made with medium-roast coffee. Espresso drinks are typically made using medium- to dark-roast coffee.

- Note that you can usually find the roast level of a coffee on the label.

Maybe you don't know which roast level you prefer. It can be helpful to ask a barista what the roast level of your favorite coffee is and they can direct you to the correct coffee product found in store or on their website.

There are no rules when it comes to personal preference. If you love a darker-roast, extra-bold cold brew, absolutely use a darker-roast coffee. If you prefer a brighter, more fruity pour-over, use a lighter-roast coffee.

When it comes to espresso, you can use any beans or grounds you like. Choose a coffee based on the flavor notes, roast level, and coffee origin you prefer rather than searcing for the word "espresso" on the label. Some coffees may specify they are an espresso blend, but you can use this type of coffee with other brewing methods as well.

QUESTION 3: DO I OWN A GRINDER?

- If you do own a grinder, I recommend buying whole beans to grind fresh at home. Freshly ground coffee tastes fresher, and grinding the beans yourself gives you full control over the grind size so you can use the coffee for different brewing methods, if desired.
- If you don't own a grinder, I recommend buying ground coffee. The taste of the coffee won't be as fresh, but it eliminates the need for an extra step when making your coffee at home. Many grocery stores provide grinders in the coffee aisle, and you can adjust the grind from coarse to fine. You could even ask your local coffee shop if they're able to grind beans for you.

QUESTION 4: WHAT TYPE OF COFFEE IS NEEDED FOR THE MACHINE OR BREWING METHOD I OWN?

A big consideration when buying coffee is the machine or brewing method you will use. If you have a Nespresso machine, you need to buy Nespresso pods; a bag of coffee beans will be useless to you. For an espresso machine, you need whole beans if you have a grinder at home, or finely ground coffee if you do not. Keep in mind, though, that a coarser pre-ground coffee (like many options from the grocery store) may be too coarse for your machine and you may experience issues with your espresso extractions.

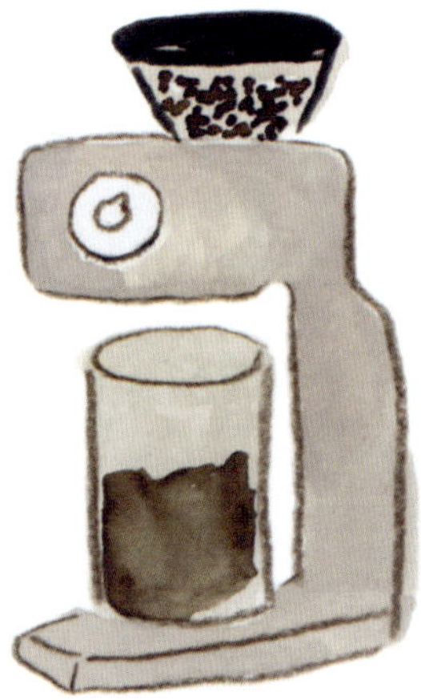

CHOOSING YOUR COFFEE

Here's a list of factors to consider when buying coffee. Decide which are most important to you.

ORGANIC

Organic coffee is made from beans that are grown and processed without synthetic fertilizers or chemicals, using environmentally friendly practices. Look for the USDA Organic seal or certification on the bag of coffee, or ask a barista if they have any organic coffee options.

AFFORDABILITY

If a big priority for you is finding the most cost-effective coffee option, consider buying from a bulk foods store like Costco. You can get large boxes of K-Cups or large bags of beans or grounds. Keep in mind this won't be the freshest-tasting option, but it will be budget-friendly. Another option is a grocery outlet store. These stores sell products at a discounted price if the package is slightly damaged or if the product is nearing its best-by date.

FRESHLY ROASTED

Freshly roasted coffee or roast-to-order coffee will give you the freshest-tasting coffee at home. Many coffee shops offer roast-to-order coffee that you can order online. This is a great choice if you're willing to pay a bit more per bag than at a grocery store, and in many cases, you can get your coffee delivered right to your home or workplace.

FLAVOR NOTES

We all gravitate toward certain flavor notes in our coffee. For some it's sweet, chocolatey notes, and for others it's woody, smoky ones. Some coffees include flavor notes on the packaging so you can select based on which notes you enjoy most. If you value obvious or pronounced flavor notes, look for coffee that clearly lists those flavor notes.

AVAILABLE IN BULK

As I mentioned above, buying coffee in bulk is a great way to save money. It's also great if you need to make coffee for bigger groups for vacations, family gatherings, or parties.

WHOLE-BEAN OR PRE-GROUND COFFEE

Depending on your preference and whether you own a grinder, pay attention to the grind size of the coffee you're buying. If you own a grinder, you can buy whole beans and grind them yourself. If you do not own one, you'll need to buy ground coffee or find another way to grind the beans. Note that pre-ground coffee will go stale faster than whole-bean coffee, so if freshness is of utmost importance to you, I recommend selecting whole-bean coffee and grinding it yourself as needed.

FAIR TRADE

The Fair Trade label is the most widely recognized ethical certification in the world. When you see a Fair Trade label on coffee, it means the beans are grown according to strict standards that promote fair treatment of farmers, support their communities, and protect the environment. Look for the Fair Trade label on bags of beans or on coffee roasters' websites.

ORIGIN

Where a coffee is from plays a large role in what it tastes like. Learn about the regions and countries where coffee beans are sourced (e.g., Ethiopia, Colombia, or Brazil) and what that means for their distinctive flavor profiles (because of soil, altitude, rainfall, and climate, for example). If you have a preference, you can look for coffees from your preferred origins or intentionally select coffees from various locations to explore new coffees from different parts of the world.

Knowing if a coffee is single-origin or a blend can also help you determine which beans to buy. Single-origin coffees can be traced back to a single, identifiable geographic location, such as a specific farm, cooperative, or region. For example, you might come across a bag coffee that is labeled "Indonesia Mt. Ijen," signifying that the coffee comes specifically from there. Single-origin coffees have certain distinguishable characteristics and flavor profiles that are specific to the region they were grown in, which means that each single-origin coffee will taste different from the next. Coffee blends combine beans from multiple origins for a consistent, balanced flavor.

Neither one of these options is better than the other—it is entirely up to you and your own preference. If single-origin coffees are important to you, you can search for them online, or find a coffee roaster that offers single-origin coffees.

PROCESSING METHOD

How a coffee is processed will affect its taste. The main processing options include natural, washed, and honey, and all have distinct characteristics (page 23). Many specialty coffee shops offer various options across these three categories so you can explore different coffees and determine your favorite processing method. Most grocery store coffees do not provide information about the processing methods used, so if shopping there, you may need to check the brands' websites.

ROAST LEVEL

Most coffees include the roast level on the bag. Look for light, medium, or dark roast depending on your preference.

ROAST DATE

A roast date, referring to when the coffee beans were roasted, is different from a best-by/expiration date or freshness date. If freshness is a priority for you, opt for coffees that provide a roast date, and look for a date as close to the current date as possible. This will give you a more precise idea of how fresh the coffee is. Most coffees sold at grocery stores have only a best-by date, not a roast date. This means you have no idea when those beans were roasted, and thus you have no idea how old the beans are.

Many small coffee shops do include the roast date on their bags of beans, and you can also find coffee roasters online that roast to order and ship to your home. (Note that you don't want to use beans that have been roasted that same day. For optimal taste, it's better to wait three to five days—and then use the beans as quickly as possible.) Beans lose their freshness as they get older, so you may discover that you prefer to buy smaller bags of beans more frequently to ensure they are at peak freshness.

BOTTLED COFFEES

There are many bottled coffees on the market nowadays, and I love it. You can find just about any coffee type, roast, or origin in bottled form, whether you're traveling, don't have a machine of your own, or just appreciate the convenience. I know it's easy to gravitate toward one favorite option, but I encourage you to try a new one here and there. You can buy a single-serving bottled or canned cold brew before committing to a larger container, or as a way to taste different flavored coffees.

YOUR QUICK BUYER'S-GUIDE CHECKLIST

If you're feeling a bit lost with all these choices, the most basic things to look for when deciding on a coffee are:

1. **Roast level:** light, medium, or dark
2. **Grind size:** Do you want a fine grind for espresso or a coarse grind for cold brew, or do you want whole beans to grind yourself at home?
3. **Flavor notes:** Look for words like "fruity," "nutty," "chocolatey," and so forth, depending on your preferences.
4. **Roast date:** Not all coffees include a roast date, but if this is an option, look for the bags with the most recent roast date.

WHERE TO BUY COFFEE

Now it's time to decide where you will buy your coffee.

LOCAL COFFEE SHOPS OR COFFEE ROASTERIES

If you often buy coffee from a local coffee shop, consider buying their beans (or grounds) to make your coffee at home. I love exploring the local coffee shops—especially ones that roast their own coffee—when I travel and buying their beans to bring home with me. Many coffee shops and roasteries sell their coffee beans online so you can still enjoy the same taste at home. These options may be more expensive than what you'd find at the grocery store, but they will usually be fresher tasting (and will often list the roast date).

LARGER CHAIN COFFEE SHOPS (STARBUCKS, DUNKIN', PEET'S, ETC.)

Most chain coffee shops sell their beans and grounds so you can make your own coffee at home. You can ask them to grind whole beans for you if you don't have a grinder at home.

GROCERY STORES

Grocery stores have an abundance of coffee options to choose from. You can select beans, grounds, Nespresso pods, K-Cups, bottled or canned coffees, or instant powders, depending on your preferred brewing method. Keep in mind, though, that while these will often be more affordable than buying from a local coffee shop or roaster, most of them will be less fresh, with few to none having a roast date listed.

AMAZON

Amazon, of course, is a super-convenient way to order coffee. As with grocery stores, you can find a variety of coffee types, but not all of them will be fresh or list a roast date. Some coffee brands have partnered with Amazon to make their products more accessible, so it's a great option to explore coffees from different cultures, like Vietnamese or Turkish coffees, that you may not be able to find elsewhere.

ONLINE COFFEE SHOP WEBSITES

Most coffee brands have their own websites where you can order their coffee directly. Keep in mind that many of them impose shipping costs unless you reach a certain payment threshold, but shopping for coffee on these websites may ensure that you're getting the freshest-possible coffee. I recommend looking for "roast to order" options; because since the coffee won't be roasted until you order it, you are usually guaranteed to get very fresh coffee.

KAT'S FAVORITE COFFEES

COLD BREW	ROAST LEVEL	FLAVOR NOTES	ORIGIN	WHERE TO BUY
Bizzy Organic Cold Brew Coffee Smooth & Sweet Blend-Coarse-Ground Coffee	Medium	Sweet, caramel, hazelnuts	100% organic Arabica coffee from Central and South America	bizzycoldbrew.com, Amazon, Walmart, Sprouts
Bizzy Organic Cold Brew Coffee-Espresso Blend—Cold Brew Bags	Medium to dark	Chocolate, berry, brown sugar	100% organic Arabica coffee from Central and South America	bizzycoldbrew.com, Amazon, Walmart, Sprouts
SToK Unsweet Black Cold Brew Coffee	Medium	Dark chocolate, graham cracker	Arabica-based blend	stokbrew.com, most chain grocery stores (Walmart, Target, Kroger, etc.)
SToK Espresso Blend Unsweet Black Cold Brew Coffee	Dark	Chocolate, nutty, dried fruit, caramel	Arabica-based blend	stokbrew.com, most chain grocery stores (Walmart, Target, Kroger, etc.)

ESPRESSO BEANS	ROAST LEVEL	FLAVOR NOTES	ORIGIN	WHERE TO BUY
Press Coffee -Spitball Espresso Blend	Light	Strawberry, chocolate, creamy	Columbia 60%, Ethiopia 40%	presscoffee.com and Press Coffee locations (AZ)
Press Coffee-Twitch Espresso Blend	Medium	Cherry, dark chocolate, sweet	Nicaragua 66%, Mexico 34%	presscoffee.com and Press Coffee locations (AZ)
Sightglass Coffee-Organic Owl's Howl	Medium	Cacao nibs, stone fruit, candied orange peel	Central America and East Africa	sightglasscoffee .com
Blue Bottle Coffee Espresso	Medium-dark	Chocolate, nougat, brown sugar	Latin America, Africa	bluebottlecoffee .com, Target, Amazon

INSTANT COFFEE POWDERS	ROAST LEVEL	FLAVOR NOTES	ORIGIN	WHERE TO BUY
Nescafé Gold-Instant Espresso Blonde Coffee	Light	None specified	Ethiopia, Brazil, Vietnam	nescafe.com, Amazon, most chain grocery stores
Café Bustelo-Instant Espresso Powder	Dark	None specified	None specified	cafebustelo.com, most chain grocery stores, Amazon

NESPRESSO PODS	ROAST LEVEL	FLAVOR NOTES	ORIGIN	WHERE TO BUY
Double Espresso Dolce	Medium	Caramel, malted cereal	Uganda	nespresso.com, Amazon
Melozio	Medium	Sweet, honey, cereal	Brazil	nespresso.com, Amazon
Melozio Decaf	Medium	Sweet, honey, cereal	Brazil	nespresso.com, Amazon
Peru Organic	Medium	Toasted cereal, fruity	Andes Mountains, Peru	nespresso.com, Amazon

STORING COFFEE

To maximize freshness for coffee beans or grounds, store them in an airtight container in a cool, dark, dry place. You want the coffee to have minimal exposure to light, heat, air, and moisture. **Yes, that means get those coffee beans out of your fridge.** The fridge is a too-humid environment for coffee, and the coffee can absorb odors from the foods inside.

Leave the coffee in the bag it came in if the bag can be zipped closed, or store it in an opaque airtight container on the counter or in the cupboard for up to 4 weeks. If you use a clear container, like a Mason jar, keep it in a dark place such as the cupboard (I know coffee beans look nice in clear jars on the counter, but an opaque container is a better storage option).

If you buy coffee that you don't plan on using within 4 weeks, you can vacuum-seal it and store in the freezer until ready to use. Make sure to store it in small batches, only enough for 5 to 7 days, since it will go stale faster once it's been frozen. Remove the coffee from the freezer and allow it to thaw, then grind and use. I don't recommend storing coffee for daily use in the freezer because the beans will be exposed to moisture every day when you open the bag of frozen coffee. Instead, when you're ready for a batch, thaw it, then store it in a cool, dry place, and use within a week.

BREWING METHODS

GRIND SIZE AND LEVEL

The grind size of a coffee refers to how fine or coarse it is after grinding. Grind size is important when it comes to the different brewing processes, because it affects how well or how poorly the coffee is extracted, which translates directly to how good or bad your coffee will taste. Different brewing methods require different grind sizes for the best results.

To adjust the grind size of your coffee, you have various options:

1. If you don't have a grinder, when you buy a bag of beans from your coffee shop, ask the barista if they can grind the beans for you. Make sure to specify which brewing method you plan to use them for so they can grind the coffee accordingly. However, you lose out on some of the taste and experience of freshly roasted coffee as the beans will become stale much more quickly once they're ground.

2. Grind the beans yourself at the grocery store. If you do this, I recommend buying the beans in small batches since the coffee will become stale more quickly.

3. Buy pre-ground coffee at the grocery store or order it online, but keep in mind that pre-ground coffee becomes stale faster than whole beans.

4. Better yet, buy a grinder. You can purchase a hand grinder or an electric one at some grocery stores or online, and many of these are rather affordable. This way, you can grind the beans fresh before each extraction, for the best-tasting coffee.

5. Buy a machine with a built-in grinder. Many espresso machines and coffee brewers now offer machines with grinders attached so you don't need to purchase two separate products.

CONICAL GRINDERS VERSUS FLAT BURR GRINDERS

The most popular coffee grinders are conical or flat burr grinders. Burrs are metal or ceramic serrated discs or rings that crush and grind beans between them. Conical burr grinders have a cone-shaped burr that rotates within a stationary ring-shaped burr. The beans are fed in from above and ground between the two burrs, which have rigid angled edges that crush the beans as they move down. Flat burr grinders use two parallel disk-shaped burrs, one stationary and one that rotates. The beans are fed in and ground between the sharp opposing teeth of the burrs; the coffee is broken down more and more as it's pushed out through the edges of the burrs.

When selecting the best coffee grinder for your needs, the choice is entirely up to you and your budget. Here are some pros and cons to consider with either type of grinder.

CONICAL GRINDERS	PROS	CONS
	Affordable for at home use	Less consistent/uniform than flat burr griders
	Quiet	
	Versatile brewing methods	
	Better coffee body and texture	

FLAT BURR GRINDERS	PROS	CONS
	Consistent/uniform grind size	More expensive than conical grinders
	Versatile enough for any brewing method	Noisy
	Reduced body and increased clarity in coffee	More coffee retention
		Harder to clean than conical grinders

CONICAL BURR

FLAT BURR

There is also a third category of grinders, blade grinders. Rather than a burr, these have a blade that spins around to chop or grind the coffee beans. Blade grinders are the most affordable option, but they are limited in their grinding ability—with blade grinders, you'll get an inconsistent grind. You could use a blade grinder if you're making cold brew or even drip coffee in a coffee maker, but for the best-possible extraction across all the different brewing methods, I recommend a conical or flat burr grinder.

While I understand not everyone has the desire or time to grind their coffee beans fresh every morning, it is a practice that I believe can immensely improve your at-home coffee experience. Coffee beans' flavors and freshness fade over time, and when the coffee is pre-ground, it loses flavor and freshness even faster. Freshly grinding coffee helps retain its natural oils and aromatic compounds, resulting in a fuller, more flavorful cup. Plus, using whole beans allows you to control the grind size so you can customize and adjust your extraction no matter which brewing method you're using.

Here are a few examples of how the grind size affects the overall extraction of various brewing methods.

COARSE

MEDIUM

FINE

COARSE GRIND

French Press—This uses an immersion brewing process, which means coffee grounds are steeped or immersed in hot water for several minutes. Since the grounds are in direct contact with the water for a longer period of time than for other methods, using a coarse grind is recommended to slow down the extraction and help prevent the coffee from becoming too bitter.

Cold Brew—For cold brew coffee, a coarse grind is recommended because the grounds are immersed in cold water for a longer brewing time. A coarse grind ensures a slower, more even extraction as the water gently pulls out the desirable flavors without harshness or bitterness.

MEDIUM GRIND

Drip Coffee—For automatic drip coffee makers, like a traditional coffee pot, a medium grind is ideal as it allows the water to easily drip down through the coffee grounds into the carafe or pot below, resulting in a balanced, even extraction.

MEDIUM-FINE GRIND

Single-Cup Pour-Over—This refers to a small-batch brewing method whereby you pour the hot water over the coffee grounds in a filter and allow the water to seep down through the coffee into the cup. A medium-fine grind is recommended here so the flow is slow, giving the coffee plenty of time to be extracted.

AeroPress—This is a manual coffee brewer that uses air pressure to force the water through the grounds. A medium-fine grind allows the AeroPress to build up more pressure and resistance as the water is pressed through the grounds, resulting in a balanced, even extraction.

Vietnamese Phin Filter—This is a single-serve brewing device where the hot water is poured over the coffee grounds inside a phin filter brew chamber, and the liquid percolates through a metal filter into the cup underneath. A medium-fine grind allows the water to flow through the coffee and filter at a moderate pace, for an even, balanced extraction.

FINE GRIND

Espresso—To get a full, rich flavor in a short amount of time, a fine grind is ideal for espresso because it creates a greater resistance aginst the flow of water, allowing enough flavor to be extracted from the coffee during the fast brew.

BEST PRACTICES, TOOLS, AND TIPS

Familiarizing yourself with the full range of brewing methods is one of the keys to making all types of great coffee at home. This section covers how brewed coffee is different from cold brew or espresso and beyond, and which processes are used to make various coffee-shop drinks at home.

FILTER COFFEE (PERCOLATION BREWING)

Filter coffee is made by pouring hot water through a bed of coffee grounds and a filter, which separates the brewed coffee from the grounds.

POUR-OVER (MANUAL DRIP COFFEE METHOD)

For this method, the hot water is poured over a bed of ground coffee in a cone-shaped brewer. Gravity pulls the water down through the coffee grounds so the coffee slowly drips down into a vessel below.

Recommended Variables (or adjust according to your preference):

- 20 grams ground coffee, 320 grams water (1:16 ratio)
- Water temperature: 200° to 205°F
- Medium-fine grind

Pros: rich and full-bodied flavor; customization; compact and portable; affordable; equipment longevity; environmentally friendly; full control over pour speed, water temperature, and brew time

Cons: longer brew time; requires extra tools; requires more skill and precision with pouring technique; single-serving only (although this could also be a pro)

Difficulty: 3/5

METHOD:

1. Heat the water to 200° to 205°F in a gooseneck kettle. Set the pour-over brewer over a mug and place the paper filter in the brewer. Rinse the filter with hot water, pour the hot water out of the mug, and set the brewer back on top.

2. Weigh out the coffee beans and grind to a medium-fine grind, then place the grounds in the filter. Shake the brewer to even out the grounds.

3. Using a gooseneck kettle, slowly pour in just enough water to dampen all of the grounds. When pouring, start in the center and move outward, using a circular motion.

4. Carefully lift the brewer above the mug, and gently swirl it in a circular motion to fully mix the coffee and water. Set the brewer back on top of the mug and let the coffee sit for 30 to 40 seconds. The coffee will bloom, and you should see carbon dioxide bubble up from the grounds.

5. Once the bloom has settled, slowly pour in more water, again in a circular motion, starting at the center and gradually moving outward. Pour the water slowly and only over the grounds so it does not come in direct contact with the filter. This slow pour should use about half of the total water remaining.

6. Gently swirl the brewer to release any grounds stuck to the sides, or use a spoon to stir the grounds very gently, and then pour in the remaining water, again in a circular motion. Swirl the brewer once more, then lift it up and drop back down to settle and flatten the grounds.

7. Allow the coffee to drain fully into your mug, then discard the filter and coffee grounds. Total brew time should be 2½ to 3½ minutes.

AUTOMATIC DRIP COFFEE METHOD

For this drip coffee method, the ground coffee is added to a filter inside a machine, the hot water is poured over the top to saturate the grounds, and then the coffee drips down into a carafe below. This is the method used with most traditional coffee pots, where the water temperature and brewing time are preset and the machine automatically brews the coffee with just the push of a button.

Recommended Variables (or adjust according to your preference):

- 20 grams ground coffee, 360 grams water (1:18 ratio)
- Medium grind

Pros: set it and forget it; consistent and reliable taste; affordable; minimal effort; no specific skills or techniques required; customizable coffee-to-water ratio; can brew large batches

Cons: inability to control extraction aspects like water temperature, pour speed, and brew time; harder to keep clean, requires paper filters; plastic components

Difficulty: 1/5

METHOD:

1. Fill the coffee pot water reservoir with the water.

2. Weigh out the coffee beans and grind to a medium grind. Place a paper filter inside the machine, then add the coffee grounds to it.

3. Press the Start button to begin the brewing process and allow the coffee to drip into the vessel below.

AEROPRESS

An AeroPress is a manual coffee brewer that uses air pressure to force the water through the coffee grounds for a smooth, full-bodied coffee.

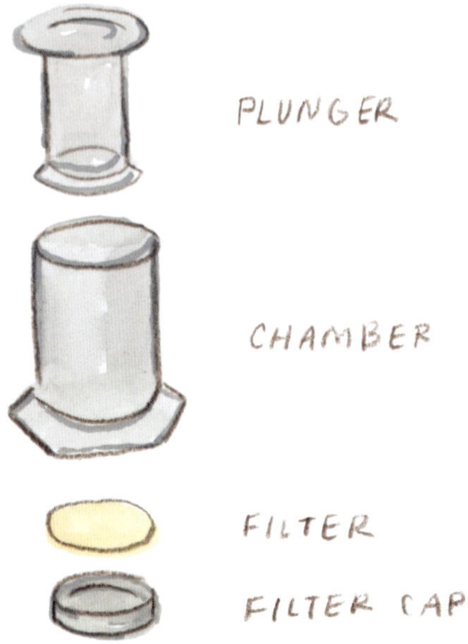

Recommended Variables (or adjust according to your preference):

- 18 grams ground coffee, 220 grams water (1:12 ratio)
- Water temperature: 185°F
- Medium-fine grind

Pros: compact and portable; lightweight; quick brew time; affordable; easy to use; customizable strength; last a long time; velvety-smooth, rich, full-bodied flavor; less bitterness

Cons: small brewing capacity; requires paper filters; plastic components

Difficulty: 2/5

METHOD:

1. Weigh out the coffee beans and grind to a medium-fine grind, then heat the water to 185°F in a kettle or a pot.

2. Place the paper filter in the filter cap and lock the cap onto the AeroPress chamber. Set the chamber on top of a mug.

3. Add the coffee grounds to the chamber, shake gently to level the coffee, and then pour the hot water over the grounds to saturate them and stir gently for 5 seconds.

4. Add the plunger to the chamber, but do not plunge it down. This will create a vacuum and prevent the liquid coffee from dripping through. Let the coffee brew for 2 minutes.

5. Grab the plunger with one hand and the chamber in the other, lift the AeroPress off the mug, and very gently swirl the brewer to break the crust formed on top of the coffee. Set the AeroPress back on top the mug, and let the coffee brew for another 30 seconds.

6. Very slowly and gently press the plunger down until the plunger is touching the coffee and you can't press it down further. You should hear a hissing sound, and the press should take 30 seconds total.

7. Remove the AeroPress from the mug and discard the grounds and filter.

PHIN FILTER

A phin filter refers to a drip coffee maker used primarily in Vietnam. Phin filters produce a bold, full-bodied coffee that is often combined with sweetened condensed milk for a traditional Vietnamese coffee.

Recommended Variables (or adjust according to your preference):

- 14 grams ground coffee, 28 grams water (1:2 ratio)
- Water temperature: 195° to 200°F
- Medium-fine grind

Pros: compact and portable; lightweight; affordable; easy to use; customizable coffee strength; equipment longevity; rich, full-bodied flavor

Cons: longer brew time; temperature loss during brewing; single-serving only (although this could also be a pro)

Difficulty: 2/5

METHOD:

1. Heat the water to 195° to 200°F in a kettle or a pot.

2. Place a Vietnamese phin filter on top of a mug.

3. Weigh out the coffee beans and grind to a medium-fine grind. Add the coffee to the phin, then shake to even out the grounds. Drop the gravity press on top of the coffee.

4. Pour enough of the water over the grounds (about ½ inch of water above the gravity press) to saturate them, and allow the coffee to bloom for 45 seconds.

5. Pour in the remaining water to fill the filter all the way and let it drip into the mug below. Let the coffee brew for 3 to 5 minutes, then carefully remove the phin.

IMMERSION COFFEE

Immersion coffee is made by fully steeping coffee grounds in water so they can extract evenly, and then separating the grounds from the brewed coffee.

FRENCH PRESS

For this immersion brewing process, ground coffee and hot water are combined in a brewer called a French press. The coffee is fully saturated and allowed to steep for several minutes. Then the plunger is pressed down, straining the liquid coffee through a mesh strainer, and the brewed coffee is poured out of the press.

Recommended Variables
(or adjust according to your preference):

- 30 grams ground coffee, 500 grams water (1:16 ratio)
- Water temperature: 200° to 210°F
- Coarse grind

Pros: rich and full-bodied flavor; customization; compact and portable; affordable; equipment longevity; environmentally friendly; full control over water temperature and brew time

Cons: coffee sediment may remain; can easily be overextracted if not watched; harder to clean; less suitable for larger batches

Difficulty: 2/5

METHOD:

1. Weigh out the coffee beans and grind to a coarse grind, and add to the French press.

2. Heat the water to 200° to 210°F in a kettle or a pot, and pour it over the coffee grounds.

3. A crust will form on top of the coffee: use a spoon to gently stir and break it up, then use a spoon to scoop out any foam or ground coffee bits floating on top and discard.

4. Let the coffee brew for 4 to 5 minutes, then place the plunger lid on top of the brewer and press down until the mesh strainer touches the top of the liquid coffee. Do not press the plunger all the way down to the bottom of the brewer or you will get grainy bits of grounds in your coffee.

5. Slowly pour the brewed coffee into a mug. Keep in mind that the last bit of the liquid coffee will have the most coffee ground particles, or sediment, so don't pour out all the liquid into a mug; leave the last ½ to 1 ounce of liquid inside the press.

PRESSURE COFFEE

Pressure coffee is made by pushing hot water through coffee grounds under pressure, resulting in a fuller-bodied, more concentrated coffee.

MOKA POT

A Moka pot is a stovetop–coffee maker that uses the pressure of the steam from water boiled in the lower section of the brewer that passes up through coffee grounds in the middle chamber to push the brewed coffee into the highest chamber.

Recommended Variables (or adjust according to your preference):

- 30 grams ground coffee, 300 grams water (1:10 ratio)
- Water temperature: 212°F
- Medium-fine grind

Pros: compact and portable; affordable; rich and robust flavor; easy to use; eco-friendly; customizable strength; equipment longevity

Cons: requires careful monitoring; brewer gets very hot; easy to result in overextracted bitter or burnt coffee

Difficulty: 3/5

METHOD:

1. Heat the water to 212°F in a kettle or a pot, and add it to the pot base to just below the safety valve.

2. Weigh out the coffee beans and grind to a medium-fine grind. Add the coffee grounds to the funnel filter and tap it gently on the table so that the coffee is evenly distributed: do not compact the grounds.

3. Place the funnel filter on top of the pot base.

4. *Optional:* If desired, place a round AeroPress paper filter underneath the top chamber piece for an extra layer of filtration.

5. Use a towel or oven mitt to hold the base in place and screw on the top of the pot until fully sealed.

6. Place the pot on a burner, without closing the lid, and heat over medium-low heat until the coffee begins flowing up into the top chamber.

7. Lower the heat slightly; you want a slow and steady brew. If the coffee is sputtering out ferociously, remove the brewer from the burner until it calms down, and then return it to the heat.

8. Allow the coffee to continue flowing into the top chamber until you see it sputtering and bubbling out, then carefully remove the pot from the heat.

9. Serve the coffee immediately, or pour into a carafe; do not leave the coffee inside the Moka chamber, or the residual heat will negatively affect its taste and flavor.

10. Let the pot cool completely before disassembling and cleaning it.

ESPRESSO

Espresso is a strong, highly concentrated coffee that is made by forcing water through tightly packed, finely ground coffee at high pressure.

SEMIAUTOMATIC ESPRESSO MACHINE

A semiautomatic espresso machine is a coffee brewer that uses a pump to automate the temperature and pressure control, while often allowing the user to manage the grind size, tamp, and extraction time.

Recommended Variables (or adjust according to your preference):

- 18 grams ground coffee input, 36 grams of espresso liquid output
- 25–35 second extraction time
- Fine grind

Pros: equipment longevity; long-term cost savings

Cons: expensive up-front cost; steep learning curve

Difficulty: 4/5

METHOD:

1. Add water to the water reservoir and turn on the machine.

2. Weigh out the beans and add them to the hopper. Place the single-wall double-shot basket inside the portafilter, and then screw the dosing funnel onto the portafilter. Grind the beans into the basket, stopping when you hear a loud screeching sound, indicating there are no beans left in the hopper. (Depending on your machine, you may be able to program the machine to give you a set amount of grounds each time if desired.)

3. Set the portafilter down on the counter and use an espresso stirrer (or a Weiss Distribution Technique tool) to stir the grounds. Make sure you get into the edges and to the bottom of the portafilter, and break up any clumps or release any air pockets. Give the portafilter a gentle tap to level the grounds and remove the dosing funnel.

4. Use a distributor tool to spread the grounds out evenly, then flip the tool over to tamp down the grounds. Press it down firmly and evenly to compact the grounds into a puck. Lock the portafilter into the machine under the group head. Press the double-shot button for a double shot of espresso.

Note that the following methods do not produce true espresso but will make a more concentrated coffee product than a cup of traditional brewed coffee, and can be used to make espresso-style drinks like lattes, mochas, shaken espressos, etc.

INSTANT ESPRESSO POWDER

• Combine the espresso powder with warm water in a cup and stir or whisk until the powder is fully dissolved.
• I recommend using 1 teaspoon of instant espresso powder with 1 ounce of warm water for every shot of espresso.

KEURIG MACHINE & K-CUPS

• Place a K-Cup in the Keurig machine and select the Shot function to brew about 4 ounces of liquid.
• I recommend using a 1:1 ratio of espresso to milk for your Keurig espresso drinks.

NESPRESSO MACHINE & ESPRESSO PODS

• Fill the water reservoir with water, and then place an espresso or double-espresso Nespresso pod inside the Nespresso machine and press Start to brew.

MOKA POT

• Follow the Moka pot instructions on page 55 using 18 to 20 grams of coffee and 120 grams boiling water.

AEROPRESS

• Follow the AeroPress instructions on page 52 using 18 to 22 grams of coffee and 75 to 80 grams of boiling water. Brew for 30 seconds before inserting the plunger and pressing it down slowly.

FRENCH PRESS

• Follow the French press instructions on page 54 using 18 grams of medium-fine ground coffee and 36 grams of hot water (195° to 205°F).

COLD BREW

Cold brew is made by steeping coarsely ground coffee and room-temperature water at room temperature for 12 to 24 hours.

FRENCH PRESS METHOD

Recommended Measurements:

• 1½ cups coarsely ground coffee and 24 ounces room-temperature water, plus more water after the coffee is brewed. Note this ratio creates a cold brew concentrate, which you will need to dilute with more water once the coffee is brewed.

METHOD:

1. Add the coffee and water to the French press and stir until all the grounds are saturated.

2. Place the plunger inside the press, but don't plunge it down yet. Set the French press on the counter and let the coffee steep for 18 to 20 hours.

3. After steeping, slowly press down the plunger and then pour out the cold brew. Keep in mind that the last bit of the liquid coffee will have the most coffee ground particles, or sediment, so don't pour out all the liquid, leave the last ½ to 1 ounce of liquid inside the press.

4. This produces a cold-brew concentrate, to be diluted with cold water. I like a 1:2 ratio of concentrate to water. So, for example, if you have 16 ounces of concentrate, add 32 ounces of cold water. Or add 6 ounces of the concentrate to a cup and stir in 12 ounces cold water.

NUT-MILK BAG METHOD

Recommended Measurements:

• 1 cup coarsely ground coffee and 32 ounces room-temperature water

METHOD:

1. Combine the coffee and water in a large Mason jar or container and stir well.

2. Cover the jar or container and allow the coffee to steep on your counter for 18 to 20 hours.

3. Place a nut-milk bag in another jar or container and pour the coffee-infused liquid into the bag. Squeeze the nut milk bag gently to release all the liquid; discard the grounds from the bag. Seal the container and store the cold brew in the refrigerator.

COLD BREW–MAKER METHOD

Recommended Measurements:

- 1 cup coarsely-ground coffee grounds and 32 ounces room-temperature water

METHOD:

1. Put the coffee in the mesh filter of a cold brew maker and fill the contraption with the water.

2. Seal the container with a lid and allow the coffee to steep on the counter for 18 to 20 hours.

3. After steeping, remove the mesh filter and discard the coffee grounds.

4. If desired, strain the cold brew through a nut-milk bag or cheesecloth into another container or jar to remove any sediment or other deposits.

5. Seal the container and store the cold brew in the refrigerator.

COLD BREW BAG METHOD

Recommended Measurements:

- 1 cup coarsely ground coffee and 32 ounces room-temperature water

METHOD:

1. Place the coffee grounds inside a cold-brew bag, and put the filled bag in a large container or Mason jar.

2. Carefully add the water, making sure the grounds are fully immersed. Cover the container or jar and let the coffee steep on the counter for 18 to 20 hours.

3. Uncover the container or jar and squeeze the bag to release all the liquid; discard the grounds. Seal the container and store the cold brew in the refrigerator.

ICED COFFEE

A chilled coffee product made by combining hot brewed coffee (often made using a higher ratio of grounds to water to account for ice meltage) with ice cubes.

METHODS

Pour-over + ice

- Follow the pour-over brewing steps on page 50, using a 1:16 ratio of coffee grounds to water.
- Let the coffee drip over ice in a heat-proof container, or brew the coffee into a mug or carafe, fill a heat-proof drinking cup to the top with ice, and pour the hot coffee over ice to chill.

Drip coffee + ice

- Follow the drip coffee brewing steps on page 51, using a 1:15 ratio of coffee grounds to water.
- Brew the coffee into the coffee pot or carafe. Fill a cup to the top with ice and pour the hot coffee over ice to chill.
- Alternatively, you can allow the coffee to cool to room temperature and then add to a cup of ice. Keep in mind that this will change the taste since coffee loses its flavor and aromas, and becomes more bitter and acidic the longer it sits.

AeroPress + ice

- Follow the AeroPress brewing steps on page 52, using a 1:10 ratio of coffee grounds to water.
- Fill a cup to the top with ice and set the AeroPress over the cup. Plunge down to brew the coffee directly onto ice.
- Alternatively, you can plunge the coffee into a mug and allow the coffee to cool to room temperature, then add to a cup of ice. Keep in mind that this will change the taste of the coffee.

Moka pot + ice

- Follow the Moka pot brewing steps on page 54, using a 1:9 ratio of coffee grounds to water.
- Fill a cup to the top with ice and pour the hot coffee over ice.
- Alternatively, you can pour the coffee into a mug and allow it to cool to room temperature, then add to a cup of ice. Keep in mind that this will change the taste of the coffee.

French press + ice

- Follow the French press brewing steps on page 54, using a 1:15 ratio of coffee grounds to water.
- Fill a cup to the top with ice and pour the hot coffee over ice. Keep in mind that the last bit of the liquid coffee will have the most coffee ground particles, or sediment, so don't pour out all the liquid; leave the last ½ to 1 ounce of liquid inside the press.
- Alternatively, you can allow the coffee to cool to room temperature and then add to a cup of ice. Keep in mind that this will change the taste of the coffee.

Instant coffee powder + cold water + ice

- Combine ½ to 1 tablespoon instant coffee powder and 8 to 12 ounces of cold water in a 16-ounce glass.
- Stir with a spoon or froth with a handheld milk frother until the powder is fully dissolved and incorporated, then add ice to fill the cup.

Iced coffee maker

- Note that ratios and measurements will depend on the machine you are using—refer to the instruction manual for recommended ratios.
- Add the water to the water reservoir and add the coffee to the brew basket.
- Fill a cup to the top with ice and place under the brewing spout, then press the Start button to brew the coffee directly over ice in the cup.

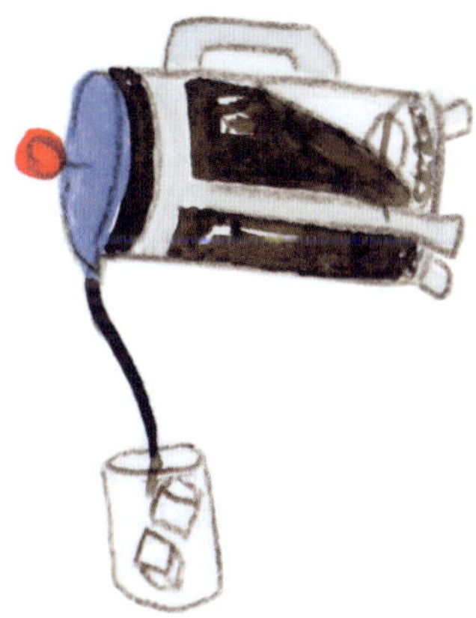

TIPS FOR MAKING THE BEST ICED COFFEE

1. Use large ice cubes.

The larger the ice cubes, the less melting and the less watered-down your coffee will be. I don't use pebble ice or nugget ice because the smaller pieces melt much more quickly.

2. Use a larger cup than you might think you need.

If you want a 16-ounce iced coffee, for example, I recommend using a 24- or 32-ounce cup filled to the top with ice. For iced coffee, the more ice the better, especially when you're pouring hot brewed coffee directly over the ice.

3. Use the "tom-tom" pouring method to chill your coffee.

My personal preference when making an iced coffee is to brew the coffee separately rather than brewing it over the ice. Once the coffee is brewed, I add my sweetener and milk or cream of choice, then pour that mixture over ice. Then I use what's called the "tom-tom" method, where you pour the coffee back and forth between the two cups—the original cup with the coffee and the second cup with the ice. Pouring back and forth between the two cups chills the coffee much more quickly and with the least amount of ice meltage. I find that four total pours are enough to chill it, and the coffee tastes significantly better than if I simply stir the coffee and ice together with a spoon.

4. Brew extra-strength coffee.

You may have noticed the ratios of coffee to water for the iced coffees are higher than those for the traditional hot brewed coffees, resulting in a stronger cup of coffee. These higher ratios allow for the inevitable meltage and dilution while still producing a strong-tasting cup. Note, however, that if you chill your hot brewed coffee before adding ice, you won't need to brew extra-strength hot coffee.

FRAPPES/BLENDED COFFEES

These are frozen coffee beverages made by blending together milk, ice, coffee, and flavored sweeteners. You'll often see them called Blended Coffees, Freezes, or Frappuccinos at coffee shops.

Recommended Measurements:

- 1 to 2 tablespoons sweetener of choice
- 8 ounces milk of choice, or as needed
- 2 teaspoons instant coffee or instant espresso powder (or ½ tablespoon coffee concentrate)
- ⅛ teaspoon xanthan gum, optional
- 1¼ cups ice cubes, or as needed

METHOD:

1. In a blender, combine the sweetener, milk, instant coffee or instant espresso (or coffee concentrate), xanthan gum (for texture), and ice cubes. Blend until smooth and creamy. If the mixture is too thick, add more milk; if it is too thin, add more ice.

2. Pour the blended coffee into a cup and enjoy.

TIPS FOR MAKING THE BEST FRAPPES

1. Use instant coffee or instant espresso powder instead of liquid coffee.

Instant powders give you a bold coffee flavor but won't water down the frappe. You could also use a coffee or espresso concentrate for the coffee flavor without adding too much liquid. But if you want to use liquid coffee, like chilled brewed coffee, cold brew, or espresso, reduce the amount of milk.

For example, instead of 8 ounces of milk, use 6 ounces of milk and 2 ounces of espresso to equal 8 total ounces. But if you're using cold brew, use 6 ounces of cold brew and 2 ounces of milk.

2. Add xanthan gum powder for a better texture.

Xanthan gum is used to thicken, stabilize, and emulsify the frappe—you only need ⅛ teaspoon powdered xanthan gum to get a creamy, homogenous texture. But even if you're doubling or tripling a frappe recipe, you'll only need ⅛ teaspoon—don't add more, or the frappe will have a gummy texture.

HOW TO STEAM MILK FOR HOT COFFEE & TEA BEVERAGES

If you've ever had a hot espresso or hot tea beverage like a cappuccino, flat white, or hot chai latte, you will be familiar with steamed milk. The steamed milk has been heated, aerated, and textured using hot air from a steam wand. When hot air is added to milk, it creates tiny air bubbles, and as those bubbles continue to warm and aerate, the milk molecules are transformed into a luxuriously velvety, smooth, cloud-like texture. Steaming milk also helps bring out more of the sweetness of the milk, for a beautifully balanced, delicious cup of coffee.

The good news is that you can get that same velvety-smooth steamed texture at home. And while the best option is to buy a machine with an attached steam wand, you can still get great warmed textured milk without a machine. Here is a walk-through of all the different methods for steaming milk.

STEAM WAND

- Add enough cold milk to a stainless steel milk-frothing pitcher to come to just below the bottom of the spout—you need to leave some room because the milk will increase in volume when steamed.
- Turn the steam wand on to purge it of any water or built-up condensation and then turn it off.
- Immediately insert the tip of the wand into the spout of the pitcher, just below the surface of the milk, and slightly tilt the pitcher to one side to create a vortex.
- Turn the steam wand back on to introduce air into the milk. This first step is called the "stretching phase," where you aerate the milk by adding tiny bubbles to it to increase, or "stretch," its volume. You want to hear high-pitched paper-tearing sounds, not high-pitched screeching. If you hear screeching, it means the wand is submerged too far in to the milk and you should raise it to just below the surface of the milk. This phase should last 5 to 10 seconds, or until you have achieved the proper amount of milk foam for the beverage you are making. Cappuccinos require a longer stretching phase than lattes or flat whites since they have a thicker layer of foam. Some plant-based milks, like almond and oat milk, require a slightly longer stretching phase for better texture.
- Next, submerge the wand deeper into the pitcher to create a whirlpool in the milk. At this point, the milk will stop increasing in volume but continue heating up. Continue steaming until the

pitcher becomes too hot to the touch, or the milk reaches a temperature of 140°F.

• Turn off the steam wand, remove the pitcher from the machine, and set it on the counter.

• Use a clean damp towel to wipe the milk off the end of the steam wand, then purge the steam wand to get rid of any milk buildup. Do not touch the steam wand, as it will be very hot.

• Gently tap the bottom of the pitcher on a flat surface a few times to break up any large bubbles in the milk, then swirl the pitcher to combine the milk and foam until the milk appears shiny and glossy, like wet paint.

• Pour the steamed milk into your drink and enjoy.

ELECTRIC MILK FROTHER (SUCH AS A NESPRESSO AEROCCINO)

• Add the cold milk to an electric milk frother, put the lid on top, and select the Hot Froth setting.

• Allow the milk to warm and swirl in the frother, then remove the lid and pour the warm frothed milk into your drink of choice.

STOVETOP + MILK FROTHER

• Add the cold milk to a saucepan and bring to a gentle simmer over medium-low heat, stirring the milk often to prevent scorching or sticking.

• When the milk has started lightly simmering and steaming, remove the saucepan from the heat and, using a handheld milk frother or a whisk, froth the milk for 60 seconds, or until it is bubbly and frothy.

• Pour the warmed frothed milk into your drink of choice.

• Note: You can also warm the milk in a mug in the microwave for 60 seconds instead of in a saucepan on the stove.

MICROWAVE + MASON JAR

• Add the cold milk to a Mason jar (do not cover it) and microwave for 60 seconds.

• Carefully remove the jar and cover it with the lid. Shake the jar for 1 to 2 minutes, or until the milk is bubbly and frothy.

• Remove the lid and pour the warm frothed milk into your drink of choice.

EXPERIMENT WITH DIFFERENT MILKS

Dairy milk and nondairy milks froth differently because of the varying protein and fat content. Whole milk has a high fat content, and it is widely used in coffee shops because of its smooth, creamy texture, which makes it great for latte art (see below). Almond milk and oat milk have a much lower fat content, so it is harder to achieve the same layer of luxurious froth with them, which, in turn, makes latte art more challenging.

For the best results, steam or froth almond milk until it reaches about 130°F. Steam or froth oat milk to 140°F for the best results.

There are many "barista style" plant-based milks on the market nowadays. These often have added fats and oils that allow them to froth up nicely for better texture and latte art.

LATTE ART

Latte art is the process of creating patterns or designs in a hot coffee beverage using the steamed milk. The great thing about latte art is you don't need fancy tools to make it. However, like any form of art, it takes patience and practice—don't expect perfection on day one!

THE DOT

Tilt the cup and hold the milk pitcher high above the cup. Slowly pour a thin, constant stream of foam into the middle of the cup. As the cup fills up, slowly turn it upright again so the liquid doesn't spill out. Stop pouring when the cup is about half to two-thirds full. Bring the tip of the milk pitcher close to the surface of the milk and espresso so it's almost touching. Slowly pour the milk into the center of the cup to create a white dot, and continute to pour until the dot becomes larger and larger and the cup is full.

THE HEART

To create a heart shape, tilt the cup and hold the milk pitcher high above the cup. Slowly pour a thin, constant stream of foam into the middle of the cup. As the cup fills up, slowly turn it upright again so the liquid doesn't spill out. Stop pouring when the cup is about half to two-thirds full. Bring the tip of the milk pitcher close to the surface of the milk and espresso so it's almost touching, and then keep pouring the milk into the center of the cup, while gently wiggling the milk pitcher side to side as you pour. When the cup is almost full, lift the milk pitcher and finish with a thin, high stream (like the beginning pour), "pulling through" the design by dragging the stream of the milk toward the thumb of the hand holding the mug to complete the heart.

THE TULIP

To create a tulip, tilt the cup and hold the milk pitcher high above the cup. Slowly pour a thin, constant stream of foam into the middle of the cup. As the cup fills up, slowly turn it upright again so the liquid doesn't spill out. Stop pouring when the cup is about half to two-thirds full. Bring the tip of the milk pitcher close to the surface of the milk and espresso so it's almost touching, and then keep pouring the milk into the center of the cup to create a white dot. Stop the pour, raise the pitcher slightly, and make a second dot just behind the first dot, then stop the pour again.

Repeat this process, creating white dots one after another. Once the cup is almost full, pour a final dot as a heart by wiggling the pitcher gently back and forth, then lift the pitcher, and pull a thin stream through the center. This final motion splits the design in half to create the tulip's symmetrical leaves.

HOW TO GET STARTED WITH AT-HOME COFFEE

STEP 1: PICK YOUR FAVORITE COFFEEHOUSE DRINK

Grab a pen and paper or open up the Notes app on your phone and write down the name of a drink order you often buy. Then list the ingredients needed to make that drink. For example, a Hot White Mocha would include: white chocolate sauce, espresso, steamed 2% milk, and whipped cream. The Starbucks, Dutch Bros, and Dunkin' apps all allow you to view the ingredients in their drinks.

STEP 2: DECIDE ON THE BREWING METHOD

Determine the brewing method you will use for the drink you're making. If it is a cold-brew beverage, select one of the methods on page 58. For an espresso-based beverage, choose one of the methods described on page 56. (Of course, if you use instant coffee or a premade coffee, skip this step.) Gather any necessary tools or other equipment required for your brewing method.

STEP 3: CHOOSE YOUR COFFEE

Now it's time to select the coffee to use: coffee beans or grounds, Nespresso pods, K-Cups, or whatever you prefer.

STEP 4: GATHER ANY OTHER INGREDIENTS

You have the coffee, now you need the flavorings, add-ins, and/or toppings. For example, for that Hot White Mocha, you need white chocolate sauce, steamed milk, and whipped cream. You can buy the white chocolate sauce or make it yourself: see the recipe for Homemade White Chocolate Sauce on page 81.

STEP 5: MAKE THE COFFEE

Weigh or measure all your ingredients, then brew the coffee and add your flavorings, milks, and toppings. And commit to improving your at-home coffee skill, one drink at a time, following the recipes for my coffee-shop level coffees, starting on page 72.

MODIFICATIONS

Making your own coffee gives you full control over the overall experience. Whether you want to make adjustments to the coffee-shop versions because of health reasons or just personal preference, these are easy modifications you can incorporate while still making great-tasting coffee drinks.

LOWER-SUGAR/LOWER-CALORIE

Opt for sugar-free homemade or store-bought syrups to reduce the sugar and calories of any coffee-shop drink, and avoid milks that have higher amounts of added sugars. Choose low-calorie toppings such as cocoa powder, cinnamon, and zero-sugar whipped topping.

DAIRY-FREE

Make any recipe dairy-free by substituting non-dairy syrups, sauces, milks, creams, creamers, and/or toppings as necessary.

HIGH-PROTEIN

Swap the regular milk for a protein shake or ultrafiltered milk to increase the protein in any drink. You could even add a scoop of protein or collagen powder for an extra protein boost.

BASIC COFFEE-RECIPE RATIOS

When you make coffee at home, you can follow the ratios below as a starting point and then adjust them to suit your taste. These basic guidelines let you create any drink you'd like by swapping the sweetener, milk, or even the brewing method. For example, if you find a vanilla latte recipe you love but prefer cold brew, just use the same ingredients and follow the cold brew ratios instead. To make a hot latte iced, use cold milk and ice instead of steamed milk, and to turn iced lattes hot, skip the ice and steam the milk before adding it to your espresso and sweetener.

HOT OR ICED LATTE

- 1 to 2 tablespoons sweetener
- 2 shots espresso
- 6 to 8 ounces milk of choice

For iced lattes, I like to follow my SEMI Method, which combines the espresso and milk (and sweetener) first to partially cool down the espresso and then adds ice. This results in a less-watered-down drink, since less of the ice will melt in the latte. Add the ingredients to your cup in the following order:

- S—Sweetener
- E—Espresso
- M—Milk
- I—Ice

COLD BREW OR ICED COFFEE

- 1 to 2 tablespoons sweetener
- 12 ounces cold brew or iced coffee
- 1 to 2 ounces cream (half-and-half or heavy cream) OR 1 to 3 ounces milk

HOT COFFEE

- 1 to 2 tablespoons sweetener
- 8 to 10 ounces hot coffee
- ½ to 1 ounce cream (half-and-half or heavy cream) OR 1 to 2 ounces milk

FRAPPE/BLENDED COFFEE

- 1 to 2 tablespoons sweetener
- 8 ounces milk of choice
- 1¼ cups ice
- ⅛ teaspoon xanthan gum, optional
- 2 teaspoons instant coffee powder, optional

COMMON ESPRESSO DRINKS

- **Americano/Long Black:** espresso + water (1:3 or 1:4 ratio of espresso to water)
- **Latte:** espresso + milk (1:3 or 1:4 ratio of espresso to milk)
- **Breve:** espresso + half-and-half (1:3 or 1:4 ratio of espresso to half-and-half)
- **Mocha:** espresso + milk + chocolate sauce (1:3 or 1:4 ratio of espresso to milk)
- **Flat white:** espresso + steamed milk (1:2 ratio of espresso to milk)
- **Cappuccino:** espresso + steamed milk with a thick layer of milk foam (1:3 ratio of espresso to milk)
- **Macchiato:** espresso + a dollop of milk foam
- **Cortado:** equal parts espresso + steamed milk (1:1 ratio of espresso to milk)
- **Espresso con panna:** espresso + whipped cream
- **Affogato:** espresso + ice cream

KAT'S TIPS

These tips reflect my hard-won lessons from years of teaching myself how to make great coffee at home.

WEIGH AND MEASURE EVERYTHING

The best way to ensure consistency with your at-home drinks, especially when you're first starting out, is to weigh or measure all the ingredients. That way, you can replicate the same drink day after day.

USE PURIFIED OR FILTERED WATER

For the best-tasting coffee, use good-quality purified or filtered water. Tap water can have chemicals that affect the flavor of your coffee or recipe. I even use purified or filtered water in my homemade syrups.

CLEAN YOUR COFFEE EQUIPMENT OFTEN

It's easy to neglect your coffee maker and just continue to expect it to perform at its highest level. But coffee makers need some TLC too, which includes giving them regular wipe-downs, emptying the drip tray regularly, washing some of the tools and pieces, and even cleaning and descaling the machine.

EXPERIMENT WITH DIFFERENT FLAVORINGS, COFFEES, AND MILKS

I used to stick to my usual flavors, milks, and coffees because I was afraid to waste money on something I might not like. Then I flipped my mindset: what if I actually loved it? That shift opened the door to countless flavor combos, brewing methods, and incredible coffees I'd never imagined enjoying (hello, Iced Blackberry Mocha; page 91). Try different beans, syrups, milks, and toppings. You won't know all your favorites until you try them.

UNDERSTAND THAT AT-HOME COFFEE TAKES PRACTICE!

Like any skill, at-home coffee takes practice. The more espresso shots you pull, the better your extractions. The more cold brews you make, the better these will taste. With time and practice (and this book), you'll get better. Repeat after me: "I don't suck at making coffee, I just have things to learn and improve."

MAKE AT-HOME COFFEE A HABIT

Making great at-home coffee takes effort at first, but the more you do it, the more it will become second nature. And then one day you'll be yawning in front of your coffee maker, wondering how you once paid $7-plus for the drink you just made for under $2.

7-DAY CHALLENGE TO JUMP-STARTING YOUR AT-HOME COFFEE JOURNEY

I challenge you to go seven days drinking only coffee you make at home. Choose one or two drinks you want to attempt at home, then gather the necessary ingredients and tools to make them. You can do it alone, or make it a challenge with your entire household or your friend group. Make it interesting, by competing and voting for the most creative coffee combo of the week!

If you're not ready to fully commit to making all your coffee at home, you can start building the habit—and saving money—by taking small steps.

- **Order a plain cold brew or iced coffee at the coffee shop and add your own syrup, caramel drizzle, milk, or cold foam.** Bring your add-ins with you so you can mix up the drink in the parking lot before work, or take the coffee home after you buy it to customize it there.
- **For lattes, buy only the espresso.** Choose the number of shots you want, then add your own milk and syrup at home.

By using coffee shop basics like cold brew, iced coffee, or espresso as your starting point, you save on pricey add-ins, control what goes in your cup, and get one step closer to confidently making your own coffee drinks.

SETTING UP AN AT-HOME COFFEE SHOP

The goal of this book is to enable you to re-create all your favorite coffee shop drinks at home by turning your own space into your favorite new café. An at-home coffee bar isn't just for your daily latte; it's a low-fuss, affordable way to host friends by offering a cozy coffee-centric gathering spot and serving some baked goods. Here's what you need to do it.

EQUIPMENT AND COFFEE

Think coffee machines and makers, grinders, milk frothers, and any other necessary equipment, as well as coffee beans, grounds, or powders. Consider having at least one iced and one hot beverage option for guests to choose from.

SEASONAL DECOR AND GLASSWARE

Add seasonal plants, artwork, and decorations (such as pumpkins during the fall or a gingerbread house for the holidays), just like a coffee shop has. Use festive mugs and glasses or get creative with other drinking vessels. A fun option is using wine or margarita glasses for iced coffee drinks to make them feel elevated and fancy.

COFFEE ADDITIONS AND TOPPERS

Keep your fridge stocked with a variety of milks, creamers, and homemade syrups and sauces so you can accommodate different taste and dietary preferences. For shelf-stable ingredients, think store-bought syrups and sauces, seasonings, and/or fun shakable toppings. Consider making homemade syrups to bottle and give guests as thank-you gifts so they can re-create the coffees you served them in their own homes.

BAKED GOODS

Serve a platter of homemade or store-bought baked goods for guests to enjoy alongside their coffee. Or maybe you can even work out a deal where guests bring a baked good to share in exchange for good company and coffee. Have fun and get creative with your coffee bar! The goal is to share your experience with others so they can see how fun and simple making coffee-shop beverages at home can be.

M O C H A S

CLASSIC MOCHA

Ahh, the classic mocha, that beloved combination of espresso and chocolate sauce with a dollop of whipped cream on top. It's like a brownie with ice cream in coffee form. And the homemade chocolate sauce is so silky and dreamy, it will leave you wondering how you ever settled for store-bought mocha anything. **SERVES 1**

1 to 2 tablespoons **Homemade Chocolate Sauce** (recipe follows) or store-bought

2 shots **espresso** (about 2 ounces) to brew

8 ounces **milk** of choice

Whipped cream (optional)

Unsweetened cocoa powder for garnish (optional)

1. Add the chocolate sauce to taste to a 12-ounce mug.

2. Using your preferred method (see page 56), brew the espresso shots directly over the chocolate sauce, then stir until combined.

3. Steam the milk using your preferred method (see page 64), then pour it over the espresso mixture.

4. Top with a generous serving of whipped cream and a sprinkle of cocoa powder, if using, and enjoy.

Make It Iced: *Using a 16-ounce glass, follow steps 1 and 2, then add cold milk and ice to the glass followed by the toppings (if using).*

Homemade Chocolate Sauce

MAKES 8 OUNCES

½ cup **granulated sugar**

½ cup **water**

1 tablespoon **maple syrup**

¼ teaspoon **kosher salt**

½ cup **unsweetened cacao powder**, or cocoa powder

½ teaspoon **vanilla extract**

1. In a small saucepan, combine the sugar, water, maple syrup, and salt. Set the pan over medium heat and whisk until the sugar fully dissolves.

2. Sift in the cacao powder and whisk until smooth and glossy, 3 to 5 minutes.

3. Remove from the heat and stir in the vanilla.

4. Use the sauce right away, or let it cool completely before transferring to an airtight container, then cover and store in the fridge for up to 2 weeks.

ICED WHITE MOCHA

I used to buy an iced white mocha from that coffee shop with the siren logo every single day until I learned how to perfect mine at home. So if you're like me and believe white mochas can do no wrong, then you're going to love being able to make this one. **SERVES 1**

1 to 2 tablespoons **Homemade White Chocolate Sauce** (recipe follows), or store-bought

2 shots **espresso** (about 2 ounces), to brew

8 ounces **milk** of choice

Ice cubes

Whipped cream (optional)

1. Add the white chocolate sauce to taste to a 16-ounce glass.

2. Using your preferred method (see page 56), brew the espresso shots directly over the white chocolate sauce, then stir until combined.

3. Add the milk and ice to the glass and stir until combined and chilled.

4. Top with a generous serving of whipped cream, if using, and enjoy.

Make It Hot: *Follow steps 1 and 2 using a 12-ounce mug, then steam or warm the milk and add it to the espresso mixture. Omit the ice, and top with whipped cream, if desired.*

Homemade White Chocolate Sauce

MAKES 12 OUNCES

4 ounces **half-and-half**

2 ounces **heavy cream**

8 ounces (1 cup) **white chocolate chips** or bar

1 tablespoon **salted butter**

½ teaspoon **kosher salt**

½ teaspoon **vanilla extract**

1. In a small saucepan, bring the half-and-half and heavy cream to a simmer over medium heat, then remove from the heat.

2. Add the white chocolate and stir until it is fully melted and the mixture is smooth.

3. Add the butter, salt, and vanilla and stir until fully melted and incorporated.

4. Pour the sauce into a Mason jar or heatproof airtight container. Use the sauce right away, or let it cool completely, cover, and store in the fridge for up to 2 weeks.

SALTED CARAMEL MOCHA

It's a well-known fact that chocolate and caramel are a match made in heaven. Just look at, for example, Twix, Rolos, and Milk Duds. I can't even count how many boxes of Milk Duds I've had in my life. Chocolate and caramel are perfect for each other, and when you add a pinch of salt to the mix to elevate the combo, and then add espresso, oh my gosh, Becky, now that's a drool-worthy concoction right there. You can make this salted caramel mocha hot or iced, it's fabulous either way, but promise me you won't skip out on the easy salted cocoa powder topping—the icing on the cake. **SERVES 1**

Pinch of **kosher salt**

1 teaspoon **turbinado sugar** (or granulated sugar)

1 teaspoon **unsweetened cocoa powder**

1 to 2 tablespoons **Homemade Salted Caramel Sauce** (recipe follows) or store-bought, plus more for topping

2 shots **espresso** (about 2 ounces), to brew

8 ounces **chocolate milk**

Whipped cream (optional)

1. In a small bowl, mix together the salt, sugar, and cocoa powder; set aside.

2. Add the salted caramel sauce to taste to a 12-ounce mug.

3. Using your preferred method (see page 56), brew the espresso shots directly over the caramel sauce, then stir until combined.

4. Steam the chocolate milk using your preferred method (page 64), then pour it over the espresso mixture.

5. Top with whipped cream, if using, more caramel sauce, and the salted cocoa powder, and enjoy.

Make It Iced: *Using a 16-ounce glass, follow steps 1 through 3, then add cold milk and ice to the glass, followed by the toppings.*

DIY Chocolate Milk: *Make your own chocolate milk by combining 1 to 2 tablespoons chocolate sauce, homemade (page 78) or store-bought, and your choice of milk. Stir until the sauce is fully blended.*

Homemade Salted Caramel Sauce

MAKES 12 OUNCES

1 cup **granulated sugar**

1 stick (8 tablespoons) **salted butter**, cut into cubes, at room temperature

6 ounces **heavy cream**, at room temperature

½ tablespoon **vanilla extract**

1 teaspoon **kosher salt**

1. In a medium saucepan, heat the sugar over medium heat, stirring occasionally until the sugar is fully melted and a dark amber color, 8 to 10 minutes.

2. Remove the saucepan from the heat and vigorously whisk in the butter, 1 tablespoon at a time. Be careful, as the mixture will bubble up.

3. Slowly add the heavy cream, whisking to combine, then add the vanilla and salt and whisk once more.

4. Pour the sauce into a Mason jar or heatproof airtight container. Use the sauce right away, or let it cool completely, cover, and store in the fridge for up to 4 weeks.

DARK CHOCOLATE CHERRY MOCHA

Every year for Christmas, I buy my mom a box of cordial cherries. Although I've done this for over a decade now, every year when I'm in the holiday candy aisle, I panic because I can't remember which she likes best, the milk chocolate or the dark chocolate. I always end up picking the dark chocolate because to me, dark chocolate cherry is the elite combo, and then on Christmas I ask her which is her actual favorite, and then I forget it again. Sorry, Mom. This mocha recipe is for all the chocolate cherry lovers in the world. I recommend using a dark cocoa powder, but if you have regular on hand, that works just fine too. **SERVES 1**

1 to 2 tablespoons **Homemade Cherry Syrup** (recipe follows), or store-bought

½ tablespoon **unsweetened dark cocoa powder** (or Dutch-process), plus more for garnish

2 shots **espresso** (about 2 ounces), to brew

8 ounces **milk** of choice

Whipped cream (optional)

1. In a 12-ounce mug, combine the cherry syrup to taste and the cocoa powder.

2. Using your preferred method (see page 56), brew the espresso shots directly over the cherry syrup, then stir until combined.

3. Steam the milk using your preferred method (see page 64), then pour it over the espresso mixture.

4. Top with a generous serving of whipped cream, if using, and a sprinkle of cocoa powder.

Make It Iced: *Using a 16-ounce glass, follow steps 1 and 2, then add cold milk and ice, followed by the toppings.*

Homemade Cherry Syrup

MAKES 10 OUNCES

1 cup fresh or frozen **sweet dark cherries**, washed if fresh and pitted

1 cup **granulated sugar**

8 ounces **water**

¼ teaspoon **kosher salt**

½ to 1 tablespoon **lemon juice**

½ teaspoon **vanilla extract**

1. In a medium saucepan, combine the cherries, sugar, water, and salt and stir well, then bring to a boil over high heat.

2. Use a potato masher to gently mash the cherries, then reduce the heat and let the syrup simmer for 10 minutes. Remove from the heat.

3. Set a strainer over a Mason jar or airtight container and carefully pour the syrup into the strainer. Reserve the mashed cherries, if desired (see Note).

4. Stir the lemon juice to taste and vanilla into the syrup.

5. Use the syrup right away, or let it cool completely, cover, and store in the fridge for up to 3 weeks.

Note: You can store the mashed cherries in an airtight container in the fridge for up to 1 week. Add them to pancakes, waffles, French toast, yogurt, oatmeal, chia pudding, or ice cream.

MEXICAN MOCHA

There are a lot of different variations of the Mexican Mocha, a fun twist on the classic version, in the world, but my absolute non-negotiables are that it has to be spiced (here I chose cinnamon and nutmeg) and a smidge spicy. My husband is Mexican and he loves spicy food, but he is happy when his tongue and face are on fire, and I am not about that life. I appreciate a bit of spice while still being able to enjoy the food or beverage. This recipe has just a pinch of cayenne to leave a slight tingle in the back of your throat without being overpowering, but feel free to skip it if you don't want any heat.

SERVES 1

2 shots **espresso** (about 2 ounces), to brew

2 tablespoons **powdered sugar**

1 tablespoon **unsweetened cocoa powder**

¼ teaspoon **ground cinnamon**, plus more for garnish

¼ teaspoon **ground nutmeg**

Pinch of **cayenne pepper**

Pinch of **kosher salt**

8 ounces **milk** of choice

1. Using your preferred method (see page 56), brew the espresso shots into a 12-ounce mug.

2. In a milk frothing pitcher (or your preferred milk steaming mechanism), combine the powdered sugar, cocoa powder, cinnamon, nutmeg, cayenne pepper, salt, and milk.

3. Steam the milk using your preferred method (see page 64), then pour it over the espresso. Top with a sprinkle of cinnamon, and enjoy.

Make It Iced: *Combine the milk and all the dry ingredients in a 16-ounce glass and froth with a handheld milk frother. Add the espresso, ice, and a sprinkle of cinnamon.*

ICED BLACKBERRY MOCHA

If you love mochas but want to something a little more fun, this iced blackberry version is a must-try. I ordered this drink at a coffee shop a couple years ago and was blown away by how beautifully the sweet and tart blackberry pairs with chocolate and espresso. Whether you make it iced or hot, I know you're going to fall in love. **SERVES 1**

½ to 1 tablespoon **Homemade Chocolate Sauce** (page 78), or store-bought

½ to 1 tablespoon **Homemade Blackberry Syrup** (recipe follows), or store-bought

2 shots **espresso** (about 2 ounces), to brew

8 ounces **milk** of choice

Ice cubes

1. Add the chocolate sauce and blackberry syrup to taste to a 16-ounce glass.

2. Using your preferred method (see page 56), brew the espresso shots over the sweeteners, then stir until combined.

3. Add the milk and ice and stir to combine. Enjoy.

Make It Hot: *Using a 12-ounce mug, follow steps 1 and 2, then steam or warm the milk using your preferred method (see page 64) and add it to the espresso mixture. Omit the ice.*

Homemade Blackberry Syrup

MAKES 10 OUNCES

1½ cups fresh or frozen **blackberries**, washed if fresh

1 cup **granulated sugar**

8 ounces **water**

¼ teaspoon **kosher salt**

1. In a medium saucepan, combine the blackberries, sugar, water, and salt and stir well, then bring to a boil over high heat.

2. Use a potato masher to gently mash the blackberries, then reduce the heat and let the syrup simmer for 10 minutes. Remove from the heat.

3. Set a strainer over a Mason jar or airtight container and carefully pour the syrup into the strainer. Reserve the mashed blackberries for another use, if desired. Use the syrup right away, or let it cool completely, cover, and store in the fridge for up to 3 weeks.

PUMPKIN–WHITE CHOCOLATE BREVE

There are very few things I love more in this world than the combination of pumpkin and white chocolate. As it stands, my current list of faves includes Cocoa (my dog), my husband and my parents, and then pumpkin–white chocolate anything. If you're one of those people who believes pumpkin does not belong in coffee, I still love you, but you're wrong. This espresso drink uses half-and-half instead of milk for an extra-rich and decadent base. Then you add both pumpkin spice sauce and white chocolate sauce for the ultimate indulgent combo, perfect for fall (or really any time of year). Imagine a mug of this with a slice of warm buttered pumpkin bread. **SERVES 1**

½ to 1 tablespoon **Homemade White Chocolate Sauce** (page 81), or store-bought

½ to 1 tablespoon **Homemade Pumpkin Spice Sauce** (recipe follows), or store-bought

2 shots **espresso** (about 2 ounces), to brew

4 to 6 ounces **half-and-half**

Whipped cream (optional)

Pumpkin pie spice for garnish (optional)

1. Add the white chocolate sauce and pumpkin sauce to taste to a 12-ounce mug.

2. Using your preferred method (see page 56), brew the espresso shots directly over the sauces, then stir until combined.

3. Steam the half-and-half using your preferred method (see page 64), then pour it over the espresso mixture.

4. Top with whipped cream and a sprinkle of pumpkin pie spice, if using, and enjoy.

Make It Iced: *Using a 16-ounce glass, follow steps 1 and 2, then add cold half-and-half and ice, followed by the toppings, if using.*

Make It Dairy-Free: *Use a dairy-free half-and-half, such as Nutpods, or swap the half-and-half for a nondairy milk of choice.*

Homemade Pumpkin Spice Sauce

MAKES 14 OUNCES

¼ cup **granulated sugar**

¼ cup packed **dark brown sugar**

¾ cup canned **pumpkin puree**

2 teaspoons **pumpkin pie spice**

¼ teaspoon **kosher salt**

1 (14 ounce) can **sweetened condensed milk**

1 teaspoon **vanilla extract**

1. In a medium saucepan, combine the granulated sugar, brown sugar, canned pumpkin, pumpkin pie spice, and salt and cook over medium heat, stirring often, until fragrant, 3 to 4 minutes.

2. Reduce the heat to low, and slowly whisk in the sweetened condensed milk until fully combined. Cook over low heat for 3 to 4 minutes, whisking occasionally.

3. Remove the saucepan from the heat and stir in the vanilla.

4. Use the sauce right away, or let it cool completely, transfer to an airtight container, and store in the fridge for up to 2 weeks.

PEPPERMINT MOCHA

I just can't say no to a good peppermint mocha. I love the taste and smell, and, ultimately, the pure joy that Christmastime brings, so I'll often whip one up midsummer just to regain enough strength to forge on through the brutal Arizona summer months. The cozy homemade peppermint syrup comes together in less than twenty minutes, and when it's paired with my foolproof homemade chocolate sauce, the duo will have you singing Christmas carols all throughout the year. For a kid-friendly or caffeine-free version of this drink, you can skip the espresso. **SERVES 1**

½ to 1 tablespoon **Homemade Chocolate Sauce** (page 78), or store-bought

½ to 1 tablespoon **Homemade Peppermint Syrup** (recipe follows), or store-bought

2 shots **espresso** (about 2 ounces), to brew

8 ounces **milk** of choice

Whipped cream (optional)

Crushed candy canes for garnish (optional)

Chocolate shavings for garnish (optional)

1. Add the chocolate sauce and peppermint syrup to taste to a 12-ounce mug.

2. Using your preferred method (see page 56), brew the espresso shots directly over the sauce and syrup, then stir until combined.

3. Steam the milk using your preferred method (page 64), then pour it over the espresso mixture.

4. Top with whipped cream, a sprinkle of crushed candy canes, and chocolate shavings, if using, and enjoy.

Make It Iced: *Using a 16-ounce glass, follow steps 1 and 2, then add cold milk and ice, followed by the garnishes, if using.*

Homemade Peppermint Syrup

MAKES 10 OUNCES

1 cup **granulated sugar**

8 ounces **water**

¼ teaspoon **kosher salt**

1 teaspoon **peppermint extract**

1. In a medium saucepan, combine the sugar, water, and salt, whisk together, and bring to a boil over high heat.

2. Reduce the heat to low and let the syrup simmer for 10 minutes.

3. Remove the saucepan from the heat and stir in the peppermint extract.

4. Use the syrup right away, or it let cool completely, transfer to an airtight container, and store in the fridge for up to 3 weeks.

ICED PROFFEE MOCHA (Protein Coffee)

The dietetics major in me had to include a protein coffee recipe in this book. I wholeheartedly support the proffee trend, because I love seeing people finding creative ways to up their protein intake every day. You can easily swap the milk in any recipe in this book with a protein milk or shake, or you could add a scoop of protein powder to your choice of milk for an additional boost. This proffee recipe is a perfect health-conscious option, while still tasting like a deliciously indulgent drink you'd order from a local coffee shop. **SERVES 1**

2 shots **espresso** (about 2 ounces), to brew

8 ounces **chocolate protein shake**

Ice cubes

Unsweetened whipped cream (optional)

Homemade Chocolate Sauce (page 78), or store-bought, for drizzling (optional)

1. Using your preferred method (see page 56), brew the espresso shots into a 16-ounce glass.

2. Add the chocolate protein shake and ice and stir until combined and chilled.

3. Top with the whipped cream and a drizzle of chocolate sauce, if using, and enjoy.

Make It Hot: *Using a 12-ounce mug, follow step 1, then steam or warm the chocolate protein shake and add it to the espresso; omit the ice. Add the whipped cream and chocolate sauce, if desired.*

CHOCOLATE ALMOND BISCOTTI MOCHA

Coffee and biscotti go hand in hand, of course, but what about a biscotti-flavored coffee? You can (and should) still dunk biscotti into this coffee, but if you don't have any on hand, you can still enjoy all the delightful flavors of that crunchy cookie. And there's no need for any fancy syrups or sauces for this drink. Pair it with a baked good such as an almond croissant or plain biscotti, and you're in for a treat. If dark chocolate isn't your thing, you can substitute milk chocolate, or white chocolate. **SERVES 1**

1 ounce **dark chocolate,** chopped

8 ounces **whole milk**

1 tablespoon **light** or **dark brown sugar**

Pinch of **kosher salt**

2 shots **espresso** (about 2 ounces), to brew

⅛ teaspoon **almond extract**

⅛ teaspoon **vanilla extract**

Cocoa powder for garnish (optional)

1. In a small saucepan, combine the dark chocolate, milk, brown sugar, and salt and bring to a low simmer over medium heat, whisking until the chocolate is completely melted and the mixture is smooth.

2. Remove from the heat and stir in the almond and vanilla extracts.

3. Using your preferred method (see page 56), brew the espresso shots into a 12-ounce mug.

4. Pour the milk mixture over the espresso, top with a sprinkle of cocoa powder, if using, and enjoy.

Make It Iced: *Follow steps 1 and 2, then allow the milk mixture to cool for at least 5 to 10 minutes. Brew the espresso into a 16-ounce glass, then add the cooled milk mixture and ice, followed by cocoa powder, if using.*

LATTES

SALTED MAPLE LATTE

I think of this as the ultimate beginner latte recipe. It uses basic ingredients to sweeten and flavor—maple syrup, cinnamon, and salt—and I guarantee you have all three of these in your kitchen right now. No fancy steps, no fancy syrups. Its perfect balance of sweet and salty flavors will have you making this coffee time and time again. And not that you'd ever get tired of this combo, but if you did, I'd recommend swapping the maple syrup with honey for another fabulous sweet and salty latte. **SERVES 1**

1 to 2 tablespoons **maple syrup**

Pinch of **kosher salt**

2 shots **espresso** (about 2 ounces), to brew

8 ounces **milk** of choice

Ground cinnamon for garnish

1. Add the maple syrup to taste and the salt to a 12-ounce mug.

2. Using your preferred method (see page 56), brew the espresso shots directly over the maple syrup, then stir to combine.

3. Steam the milk using your preferred method (see page 64), then pour it over the espresso mixture.

4. Top with a sprinkle of ground cinnamon and enjoy.

Make It Iced: *Using a 16-ounce glass, follow steps 1 and 2, then add cold milk and ice to the glass, followed by the cinnamon.*

CINNAMON COOKIE BUTTER LATTE

I don't know whose idea it was to transform Biscoff cookies into a creamy, dreamy spread, but it was a genius move. Instead of dunking Biscoff cookies into a cup of coffee (which is also a genius move), try this drink that combines the two, so every sip is a luxuriously smooth and sweet sip of cookie-butter bliss. A sprinkle of cinnamon adds another layer of flavor and spice that you didn't know you needed. **SERVES 1**

1 to 2 tablespoons **cookie butter**

⅛ teaspoon **ground cinnamon**, plus more for topping

2 shots **espresso** (about 2 ounces), to brew

8 ounces **milk** of choice

Whipped cream (optional)

Biscoff cookie for garnish (optional)

1. Add the cookie butter to taste and the cinnamon to a 12-ounce mug and microwave until the butter is melted, about 15 seconds.

2. Using your preferred method (see page 56), brew the espresso shots directly over the melted cookie butter, then stir to combine.

3. Steam the milk using your preferred method (see page 64), then pour it over the espresso mixture.

4. Top with cinnamon and, if using, whipped cream and the Biscoff cookie and enjoy.

Make It Iced: *In a blender, combine the cookie butter, milk, and cinnamon and blend until smooth. Brew the espresso shots into a 16-ounce glass, then add the cookie butter–milk mixture, ice, and cinnamon, followed by the whipped cream and cookie, if using.*

HONEY LAVENDER LATTE

I know lavender in coffee may seem like a strange combination, but I promise you, it's divine. The floral notes of the lavender coupled with the sweetness of honey are so lovely and warm, it'll make you feel like you're dancing through a field of flowers on a bright spring day. The oat milk adds a subtly sweet and creamy taste that works perfectly in this recipe. You can find flavored honeys in stores and online, so instead of using honey and lavender extract, you could use a lavender honey. **SERVES 1**

1 to 2 tablespoons **honey**

⅛ teaspoon **lavender extract**

2 shots **espresso** (about 2 ounces), to brew

8 ounces **oat milk**

1. Add the honey to taste and the lavender extract to a 12-ounce mug.

2. Using your preferred method (see page 56), brew the espresso shots directly over the honey, then stir to combine.

3. Steam the milk using your preferred method (see page 64), then pour it over the espresso mixture and enjoy.

Make It Iced: *Using a 16-ounce glass, follow steps 1 and 2, then add cold milk and ice.*

ROSE CARDAMOM LATTE

Cardamom has a warm, spicy, citrusy flavor that I feel is very underrated in the coffee world. This latte recipe is here to change that. It is made with a simple rose cardamom–infused milk that is good enough to drink alone. You can use the infused milk to make any coffee recipe, but it's perfect for elevating your matcha or chai lattes. And if you want to try a cardamom mocha combo, skip the rose petals and add 1 to 2 tablespoons of chocolate sauce (page 78). **SERVES 1**

2 shots **espresso** (about 2 ounces), to brew

8 ounces **Rose Cardamom–Infused Milk** (recipe follows)

1. Using your preferred method (see page 56), brew the espresso shots into a 12-ounce mug.

2. Steam the milk using your preferred method (see page 64), then pour it over the espresso. Enjoy.

Make It Iced: *Using a 16-ounce glass, follow step 1, then add the cold infused milk and ice.*

Rose Cardamom–Infused Milk

MAKES 8 OUNCES

¼ cup **culinary-grade rose petals**

6 whole **green cardamom pods**, crushed

11 ounces **milk** of choice

1 to 2 tablespoons **maple syrup**

1. Combine the rose petals, cardamom, milk, and maple syrup to taste in a saucepan and bring to a simmer over medium-low heat. Simmer for 10 minutes, stirring often so the milk doesn't scorch or burn.

2. Remove the saucepan from the heat and pour the mixture through a strainer into a Mason jar or pitcher; discard the rose petals and cardamom.

3. Use the infused milk right away, or let it cool completely, cover, and store it in an airtight container in the fridge for up to 1 week.

ICED ROSEMARY OAT MILK LATTE

When most of us think of rosemary, we think of cooking recipes, not coffee recipes, but I'm here to change that! This latte is botanical, herbaceous, slightly sweet, and surprisingly refreshing. The honey pairs beautifully with the earthy notes of the rosemary, and when that is combined with creamy oat milk and bold espresso? It's like your favorite comforting winter drink got a summer makeover. The infused milk is super-easy to make and totally worth the steeping time. Whether you're sipping it hot on a brisk morning or enjoying the iced version on a warm afternoon, this latte is a fun and flavorful twist to incorporate in your coffee routine. **SERVES 1**

1 to 2 tablespoons **honey**

2 shots **espresso** (about 2 ounces), to brew

8 ounces **Rosemary-Infused Oat Milk** (recipe follows)

Ice cubes

1. Add the honey to taste to a 16-ounce glass.

2. Using your preferred method (see page 56), brew the espresso shots directly over the honey, then stir until the honey is fully dissolved.

3. Add the oat milk and ice, stir until combined and chilled, and enjoy.

Make It Hot: *Using a 12-ounce mug, follow steps 1 and 2, then steam or warm the infused milk and add it to the espresso mixture. Omit the ice.*

Rosemary-Infused Oat Milk

MAKES 8 OUNCES

2 sprigs **rosemary**

9 ounces **oat milk**

¼ teaspoon **vanilla extract**

1. In a small saucepan, combine the rosemary sprigs and oat milk and bring to a gentle simmer over medium-low heat. Simmer for 10 minutes, stirring often so the milk doesn't scorch or burn.

2. Remove the pan from the heat and pour the milk through a strainer into a Mason jar or pitcher; discard the rosemary sprigs.

3. Stir in the vanilla and let the milk cool to room temperature.

4. Use the infused milk right away, or store in an airtight container in the fridge for up to 1 week.

DULCE DE LECHE LATTE

This latte blends the deep, caramelized sweetness of homemade dulce de leche with bold espresso and steamed milk for a smooth, indulgent cup that's perfect on a chilly morning or as an afternoon pick-me-up. The sauce comes together easily in the oven and adds a rich, buttery depth you just can't get from store-bought versions. It's the kind of drink that feels like a real treat but is simple enough to make whenever the craving hits. And don't worry, I won't judge you for sneaking spoonfuls of the dulce de leche when no one is looking. **SERVES 1**

1 to 2 tablespoons **Homemade Dulce de Leche** (recipe follows), or store-bought

2 shots **espresso** (about 2 ounces), to brew

8 ounces **milk** of choice

1. Add the dulce de leche to taste to a 12-ounce mug.

2. Using your preferred method (see page 56), brew the espresso shots directly over the sauce, then stir until fully combined.

3. Steam the milk using your preferred method (see page 64), then pour it over the espresso mixture. Enjoy.

Make It Iced: *Using a 16-ounce glass, follow steps 1 and 2, then add cold milk and ice.*

Homemade Dulce de Leche

MAKES 12 OUNCES

1 can (14 ounces) **sweetened** condensed milk

Hot water, as needed

1. Preheat the oven to 425°F. Pour the condensed milk into an 8 × 8 baking dish. Smooth the top with a spatula, then tightly cover the dish with aluminum foil.

2. Place the covered baking dish inside a 9 × 13 baking pan, and then fill the larger pan with enough hot water to reach halfway up the sides of the smaller dish, creating a water bath.

3. Transfer the baking dishes to the oven and bake for 1 to 2 hours, checking every 30 minutes, and adding more hot water as needed to keep it about halfway up the sides of the smaller dish. Bake until the mixture is a light to medium caramel color.

4. Carefully remove the pans from the oven, remove the foil, and whisk the dulce de leche until smooth. Use the sauce right away, or let it cool completely before transferring to an airtight container, then cover and store in the fridge for up to 2 weeks.

ICED IRISH CREAM BREVE

Back in college, my husband and I (then just dating) couldn't get enough of the Iced Kicker from Dutch Bros, a local coffee chain in Arizona. It was a sweet, indulgent mix of bold espresso, a sinful amount of half-and-half, and Irish cream syrup—our daily splurge that felt equal parts comforting and energizing. While I can't quite imagine drinking one every day now (hello, dairy), the flavor has stuck with me all these years. This homemade version featuring a Homemade Irish Cream Syrup is my way of paying tribute to that nostalgic favorite, but with a made-from-scratch spin. Oh, and my favorite hack is to use a dairy-free half-and-half. **SERVES 1**

1 to 2 tablespoons **Homemade Irish Cream Syrup** (recipe follows), or store-bought

2 shots **espresso** (about 2 ounces), to brew

6 ounces **half-and-half**

Ice cubes

Cocoa powder for garnish (optional)

1. Add the Irish cream syrup to taste to a 16-ounce glass.

2. Using your preferred method (see page 56), brew the espresso shots directly over the syrup.

3. Add the half-and-half and ice, and stir until combined and chilled. Top with a sprinkle of cocoa powder, if using, and enjoy.

Make It Hot: *Using a 12-ounce mug, follow steps 1 and 2. Steam or warm the half-and-half, then add it to the espresso mixture, followed by the cocoa powder, if using. Omit the ice.*

Make It Dairy-Free: *Use a dairy-free half-and-half, such as Nutpods, or swap the half-and-half for a nondairy milk of choice.*

Homemade Irish Cream Syrup

MAKES 10 OUNCES

1 cup **granulated sugar**

4 ounces **water**

4 ounces **brewed coffee** (hot or chilled is fine)

¼ teaspoon **kosher salt**

1 tablespoon **Dutch-process cocoa powder**

1 teaspoon **vanilla extract**

¼ teaspoon **almond extract**

1. In a small saucepan, combine the sugar, water, coffee, and salt. Sift in the cocoa powder, to remove lumps, then bring the mixture to a rolling boil over high heat, stirring to dissolve the sugar.

2. Reduce the heat to medium-low and simmer the syrup for 10 minutes.

3. Remove from the heat and stir in the vanilla and almond extracts.

4. Use the syrup right away, or let it cool completely, transfer to an airtight container, and store in the fridge for up to 3 weeks.

MEXICAN WEDDING COOKIE LATTE

Mexican wedding cookies are my absolute favorite Christmas cookie! I always reach for those powdery, crumbly, nutty pillows of deliciousness that just melt in your mouth first. (Dear future children, you can put out a plate of these cookies with a glass of milk for Santa, please, and thank you.) This latte, made with almond milk, has the same buttery, nutty flavors as the beloved traditional cookie, with a hint of cinnamon and a sprinkle of powdered sugar. Picture this: it's Christmas morning and you've already eaten all the Mexican wedding cookies, but you have this cozy latte recipe, so all is right with the world. **SERVES 1**

1 to 2 tablespoons **Homemade Butter Pecan Syrup** (recipe follows), or store-bought

¼ teaspoon **ground cinnamon**

2 shots **espresso** (about 2 ounces), to brew

8 ounces **almond milk**

Powdered sugar for garnish (optional)

1. Add the butter pecan syrup to taste and the cinnamon to a 12-ounce mug.

2. Using your preferred method (see page 56), brew the espresso shots directly over the syrup, then stir until combined.

3. Steam the almond milk using your preferred method (see page 64), then pour it over the espresso mixture.

4. Top with a sprinkle of powdered sugar, if using, and enjoy.

Make It Iced: *Using a 16-ounce glass, follow steps 1 and 2, then add cold milk and ice, followed by the powdered sugar, if using.*

Homemade Butter Pecan Syrup

MAKES 10 OUNCES

1 cup **pecan halves**

1 cup **granulated sugar**

8 ounces **water**

½ teaspoon **kosher salt**

⅛ to ¼ teaspoon **butter extract**

1. Place the pecans in a medium saucepan and toast over medium-low heat, stirring often to keep the nuts from burning, until fragrant, 3 to 5 minutes.

2. Add the sugar, water, and salt and stir until the sugar is fully dissolved. Increase the heat to high and bring the mixture to a rolling boil.

3. Reduce the heat to medium-low and simmer the syrup for 10 minutes.

4. Remove the pan from the heat and pour the syrup through a strainer into a Mason jar or heatproof container. Reserve the pecans, if desired (see Note).

5. Stir the butter extract into the syrup. Use the syrup right away, or let it cool completely, transfer to an airtight container, and store in the fridge for up to 3 weeks.

Note: To make candied pecans, spread the drained pecans in a single layer on a parchment paper–lined baking sheet and bake in the oven at 350°F for 10 to 15 minutes, stirring halfway through, until the pecans are lightly toasted and fragrant. Remove the pecans from the oven and let cool before enjoying. Store in an airtight container at room temperature for up to 1 week.

ICED BLUEBERRY VANILLA LATTE

If you're a fan of blueberry pie, you're in for a treat with this latte. It has all the classic pie flavors—blueberries, of course, plus sugar, vanilla extract, and a hint of lemon. It's as if you took the pie filling, liquefied it, and added freshly brewed espresso to create the yummiest coffee recipe, reminiscent of your grandma's blueberry pie. In case she never shared her secret recipe with you, don't worry—this latte will make you forget about the original pie. If blueberries aren't your jam, swap them with strawberries, raspberries, or blackberries. **SERVES 1**

1 to 2 tablespoons **Homemade Blueberry Vanilla Syrup** (recipe follows)

2 shots **espresso** (about 2 ounces), to brew

8 ounces **milk** of choice

Ice cubes

1. Add the blueberry vanilla syrup to taste to a 16-ounce glass.

2. Using your preferred method (see page 56), brew the espresso shots directly over the syrup.

3. Add the milk and ice, stir until combined and chilled, and enjoy.

Make It Hot: *Using a 12-ounce mug, follow steps 1 and 2, then steam or warm the milk and add it to the espresso mixture. Omit the ice.*

Homemade Blueberry Vanilla Syrup

MAKES 9 OUNCES

1½ cups fresh or frozen **blueberries**, washed if fresh

1 cup **granulated sugar**

8 ounces **water**

¼ teaspoon **kosher salt**

½ tablespoon **vanilla extract**

1 teaspoon **lemon juice**

1. In a medium saucepan, combine the blueberries, sugar, water, and salt, stir well, and bring to a boil over high heat.

2. Reduce the heat to medium-low and simmer for 10 minutes, or until the syrup has slightly thickened and turned purple.

3. Remove from the heat and pour the syrup through a strainer into a Mason jar or heatproof container. Reserve the blueberries, if desired (see Note).

4. Stir the vanilla extract and lemon juice into the syrup.

5. Use the syrup right away, or let it cool completely, transfer to an airtight container, and store in the fridge for up to 3 weeks.

Note: Store the drained blueberries in an airtight container in the fridge for up to 1 week. Add them to pancakes, waffles, French toast, yogurt, oatmeal, chia pudding, or ice cream.

CHAI LATTE

When I was in college, because we both had crazy busy schedules, my dad and I would go on coffee dates to spend time together and catch up. On one occasion, we went to a coffee shop called Ground Control, where my dad told me the hot chai lattes were incredible. I wasn't a big tea drinker, but I trusted his recommendation, and, holy buckets, it was as incredible as he said. I'd never had one so spiced and creamy, and I found myself craving it even weeks after. This recipe is an ode to the dreamiest chai I've ever had, and I know it'll become a hit in your morning tea routine too! **SERVES 1**

6 ounces **Homemade Chai Concentrate** (recipe follows), or store-bought

4 ounces **milk** of choice

Ground cinnamon or **nutmeg** for garnish

1. In a small saucepan, combine the chai concentrate and milk, bring to a gentle simmer over medium-low heat, and simmer for 5 minutes, stirring often.

2. Pour the chai latte into a 12-ounce mug, top with a sprinkle of cinnamon or nutmeg, and enjoy.

Make It Iced: *In a 16-ounce glass, combine the chilled chai concentrate, cold milk, and ice, followed by the cinnamon or nutmeg.*

Make It Dirty: *Add 1 to 2 shots of espresso to an iced or hot chai latte.*

Homemade Chai Concentrate

MAKES 30 OUNCES

2 tablespoons **whole green cardamom pods**

2 **cinnamon sticks**

8 **black peppercorns**

40 ounces **water**

1-inch piece **ginger**, thinly sliced

½ cup packed **dark brown sugar**

14 **black tea bags**

½ tablespoon **vanilla extract**

1. In a medium saucepan, combine the cardamom, cinnamon, and peppercorns. Set the pan over medium heat and stir for 3 to 4 minutes, until the spices are fragrant and slightly toasted.

2. Transfer the spices to a blender or food processor (set the pan aside) and pulse until ground to a coarse powder.

3. Return the spices to the saucepan and add the water, ginger, and brown sugar. Stir to combine, then bring to a boil over high heat.

4. Reduce the heat to low and simmer for 20 minutes.

5. Raise the heat to high and return the mixture to a boil, then remove from the heat and add the tea bags to the pan. Let steep for 10 minutes.

6. Remove the tea bags and pour the mixture through a strainer into a Mason jar or heatproof container, then stir in the vanilla extract.

7. Use the concentrate right away, or let cool completely, cover, and store in the fridge for up to 3 weeks.

GINGERBREAD LATTE

There's something magical about a warm, freshly baked gingerbread cookie. This latte captures all that cookie flavor thanks to a simple gingerbread spice milk made with molasses, brown sugar, and spices including cinnamon, ginger, and cloves. I recommend making a larger batch of the spiced milk to store in the fridge for easy gingerbread lattes or to add a little holiday magic to hot cocoa, oatmeal, or baked goods. **SERVES 1**

2 shots **espresso** (about 2 ounces), to brew

8 ounces **Gingerbread Spice–Infused Milk** (recipe follows)

Whipped cream (optional)

Ground nutmeg for garnish (optional)

1. Using your preferred method (see page 56), brew the espresso shots into a 12-ounce mug.

2. Warm or steam the infused milk using your preferred method (see page 64), then pour it over the espresso.

3. Top with whipped cream and a sprinkle of nutmeg, if using, and enjoy.

***Make It Iced:** Allow the milk to cool, then add the espresso, milk, and ice to a 16-ounce glass, followed by the toppings, if using.*

Gingerbread Spice–Infused Milk

MAKES 8 OUNCES

8 ounces **milk** of choice

1 to 2 tablespoons **dark brown sugar**

½ tablespoon **unsulfured molasses**

½ teaspoon **ground cinnamon**

¼ teaspoon **ground ginger**

⅛ teaspoon **ground nutmeg**

⅛ teaspoon **ground cloves**

⅛ teaspoon **kosher salt**

1. In a small saucepan, combine all the ingredients and whisk well. Bring to a low simmer over medium-low heat and simmer for 5 minutes, stirring often so the milk doesn't scorch or burn. Remove from the heat.

2. Use the infused milk right away, or let it cool completely, transfer to an airtight container, and store in the fridge for up to 1 week.

SPICED EGGNOG LATTE

One thing I know, I will be drinking lots of eggnog in my coffee every holiday season. If you haven't tried swapping your milk or cream for eggnog yet, what have you been doing? It's rich, it's creamy, it's decadent, and when you add a pinch of brown sugar and a swirl of cinnamon and nutmeg, you get a mind-blowing explosion of pure bliss and indulgence in a cup. But if going full "'nog" is too rich for you, I get it. Use a dairy-free eggnog or opt for half eggnog and half milk for a lighter version that still tastes incredible. **SERVES 1**

1 to 2 tablespoons **light** or **dark brown sugar**

2 shots **espresso** (about 2 ounces), to brew

4 to 6 ounces **eggnog**

¼ teaspoon **ground cinnamon**

¼ teaspoon **ground nutmeg**, plus more for garnish

Whipped cream (optional)

1. Add the brown sugar to taste to a 12-ounce mug.

2. Using your preferred method (see page 56), brew the espresso shots directly over the brown sugar, then stir to dissolve the sugar.

3. Combine the eggnog with the cinnamon and nutmeg and steam the eggnog using your preferred method (see page 64). Pour the steamed eggnog over the espresso mixture.

4. Top with whipped cream, if using, and a sprinkle of nutmeg. Enjoy.

Make It Iced: *Using a 16-ounce glass, follow steps 1 and 2, then add cold eggnog, cinnamon, nutmeg, and ice, followed by the whipped cream, if using, and a sprinkle of nutmeg.*

PUMPKIN SPICE LATTE

You either love it or you hate it. Personally, I love a good PSL because it tastes incredible, but also because at that time of year, we're no longer roasting our faces off here in Arizona (summers are brutally hot here, if you didn't know). Pumpkin spice lattes mean the weather is cooler, the leaves are changing, and it's time to rewatch *Gilmore Girls* for the umpteenth time. The Homemade Pumpkin Spice Sauce is perfectly spiced and sweet and will be a recipe you come back to time and time again. And by you, I mean me. **SERVES 1**

1 to 2 tablespoons **Homemade Pumpkin Spice Sauce** (page 94), or store-bought

2 shots **espresso** (about 2 ounces), to brew

8 ounces **milk** of choice

Whipped cream (optional)

Pumpkin pie spice for garnish (optional)

1. Add the pumpkin spice sauce to taste to a 12-ounce mug.

2. Using your preferred method (see page 56), brew the espresso shots directly over the sauce, then stir until combined.

3. Steam the milk using your preferred method (see page 64), then pour it over the espresso mixture.

4. Top with whipped cream and a sprinkle of pumpkin pie spice, if using, and enjoy.

Make It Iced: *Using a 16-ounce glass, follow steps 1 and 2, then add cold milk and ice, followed by the toppings, if using.*

TRES LECHES LATTE

I didn't grow up eating tres leches cake, but since meeting my husband, who's Mexican, I've happily been around it a lot more. It's a staple in Hispanic culture and shows up at nearly every party, graduation, and quinceañera we attend. Over the years, I've grown to really love the sweet, creamy flavors that make tres leches so special. This latte is inspired by those flavors—rich, milky, and just the right amount of sweet. It's like a slice of tres leches cake in coffee form. **SERVES 1**

1 to 2 tablespoons **sweetened condensed milk**

¼ teaspoon **vanilla extract**

2 shots **espresso** (about 2 ounces), to brew

6 ounces **whole milk**

2 ounces **evaporated milk**

Ground cinnamon for garnish

1. Add the sweetened condensed milk to taste and the vanilla extract to a 12-ounce mug.

2. Using your preferred method (see page 56), brew the espresso shots directly over the condensed milk, then stir until combined.

3. Combine the whole milk and evaporated milk and steam the mixture using your preferred method (see page 64), then pour it over the espresso mixture.

4. Top with a sprinkle of cinnamon and enjoy.

Make It Iced: *Using a 16-ounce glass, follow steps 1 and 2, then add cold whole milk, cold evaporated milk, and ice, followed by the cinnamon.*

BLACK SESAME CHAI LATTE

A couple of years ago, my favorite syrup brand, Torani, released a unique new flavor: Toasted Black Sesame. With its deep, nutty, and umami flavor profile, it was so distinct and delicious that I knew I had to give it a place in this book. This chai recipe is my ode to that underrated, warming, rich flavor. You can find black sesame paste at your local Asian grocery store or on Amazon, or sometimes labeled as black tahini or black sesame tahini at larger grocery stores. If you're looking to try something a little unexpected, this drink is a great place to start. It's equally good iced, and if you're feeling bold, try adding a shot of espresso for a "dirty" version that's next-level delicious. **SERVES 1**

1 to 2 tablespoons **black sesame paste**

1 to 2 tablespoons **maple syrup**

6 ounces **Homemade Chai Concentrate** (page 129), or store-bought

4 ounces **milk** of choice

Ground cinnamon or **nutmeg** for garnish (optional)

1. In a medium saucepan, combine the black sesame paste and maple syrup to taste, the chai concentrate, and milk and bring to a gentle simmer over medium-low heat.

2. Simmer for 5 to 7 minutes, whisking continuously, until the black sesame paste is fully dissolved.

3. Pour the latte into a mug, top with a sprinkle of cinnamon or nutmeg, if using, and enjoy.

Make It Iced: *In a blender, blend together the black sesame paste, maple syrup, chai concentrate, and milk until combined. Fill a 16-ounce glass to the top with ice cubes, pour in the chai mixture, and top with cinnamon or nutmeg, if using.*

Make It Dirty: *Add 1 to 2 shots of espresso to an iced or hot chai latte.*

MINT CHIP MATCHA LATTE

Mint and chocolate are an elite flavor combo. To the people who say it tastes like toothpaste, you don't know what you're missing. Earthy matcha pairs well with a cool hint of peppermint and the richness of homemade chocolate sauce, giving you serious mint chip energy in matcha latte form. Whether you're enjoying it hot and cozy or over ice, it's a fun, elevated way to enjoy your daily matcha. **SERVES 1**

2 ounces **water**

2 teaspoons **matcha powder**

8 ounces **milk** of choice

1 to 2 tablespoons **Homemade Chocolate Sauce** (page 78), or store-bought

⅛ teaspoon **peppermint extract**

A **mint leaf** for garnish (optional)

Cacao nibs for garnish (optional)

1. Heat the water using an electric kettle, a saucepan on the stove, or the microwave until it's hot but not boiling, 160° to 175°F.

2. Meanwhile, set a matcha sifter or a small sieve over a matcha bowl. Using a matcha scoop or a spoon, scoop the matcha powder into the sifter or sieve and use the back of the scoop (or spoon) to gently push the matcha powder through the sifter or sieve into the bowl.

3. Pour the hot water over the matcha. Use a bamboo whisk or milk frother to whisk the matcha and water together (if using a whisk, make back-and-forth motions—an M or W motion). Whisk until no lumps remain and the matcha is nice and frothy, 1 to 2 minutes.

4. Steam the milk using your preferred method (see page 64). Pour into a 16-ounce mug and add the chocolate sauce to taste and the peppermint extract and stir to combine.

5. Pour the whisked matcha over the top and stir to combine. Garnish with a mint leaf and cacao nibs, if using, and enjoy!

Make It Iced: *Follow steps 1 through 3, then, using a 16-ounce glass, add cold milk, ice, the chocolate sauce, and peppermint extract. Stir to combine, then pour in the whisked matcha, followed by the garnishes, if using.*

ICED STRAWBERRY–COCONUT CREAM MATCHA LATTE

There's just something magical about the way savory matcha pairs with sweet, juicy strawberries. Add creamy coconut milk and a thick layer of salted coconut cream cold foam, and you've got a seriously dreamy latte situation. This matcha latte is refreshing, vibrant, and as pretty as it is delicious. It's the kind of drink that feels like a little treat but is simple enough to make on any day of the week. Bonus: you can enjoy it hot or iced, depending on your mood! **SERVES 1**

½ cup fresh **strawberries,** washed and stems removed

6 ounces canned **full-fat coconut milk**

2 tablespoons **maple syrup**

2 ounces **water**

2 teaspoons **matcha powder**

Ice cubes

1½ ounces **coconut cream**

¼ teaspoon **vanilla extract**

¼ teaspoon **kosher salt**

1. In a blender, combine the strawberries, coconut milk, and 1 tablespoon of the maple syrup and blend until smooth. Strain the strawberry milk through a strainer or cheesecloth and set aside.

2. Heat the water using an electric kettle, a saucepan on the stove, or the microwave until it's hot but not boiling, 160° to 175°F.

3. Set a matcha sifter or a small sieve over a matcha bowl. Using a matcha scoop or spoon, scoop the matcha powder into the sifter and use the back of the scoop to gently push the matcha powder through the sifter into the bowl.

4. Pour the hot water over the sifted matcha, and use a bamboo whisk or a milk frother to whisk the matcha and water together (if using a whisk, make back-and-forth motions—an M or W motion). Whisk until no lumps remain and the matcha is frothy, 1 to 2 minutes.

5. To a 16-ounce glass, add ice, the strawberry milk, and then the matcha.

6. In an 8-ounce glass, combine the coconut cream, vanilla, salt, and the remaining 1 tablespoon of maple syrup and froth with a handheld milk frother until thick, 15 to 30 seconds.

7. Pour the frothed coconut cream cold foam over the latte and gently stir to combine. Enjoy.

Make It Hot: *Follow steps 1 through 4, then steam the strawberry milk and add it to a 12-ounce mug; omit the ice. Pour the prepared matcha over the steamed milk, and continue with steps 6 and 7.*

MORE

ESPRESSO

DRINKS

ICED CARAMEL MACCHIATO

This popular Starbucks drink is sweet and caramely with gorgeous ombre layers of caramel, espresso, and milk. While a traditional macchiato is made with espresso, stained or marked with a small amount of steamed milk, Starbucks stains the drink using espresso and caramel sauce. This upside down latte is sweet, simple, and well worth making at home. **SERVES 1**

1 to 2 tablespoons **Homemade Vanilla Syrup** (recipe follows), or store-bought

8 ounces **milk** of choice

Ice cubes

2 shots **espresso** (about 2 ounces), to brew

Homemade Salted Caramel Sauce (page 84), or store-bought, such as Torani caramel sauce, for drizzling

1. In a 16-ounce glass, combine the vanilla syrup to taste, the milk, and ice.

2. Using your preferred method (see page 56), brew the espresso shots into an 8-ounce cup.

3. Gently pour the espresso over the top of the flavored milk, top with a generous drizzle of caramel sauce, and enjoy.

Make It Hot: *Brew the espresso shots into an 8-ounce cup and set aside. Add the vanilla syrup to a 12-ounce mug. Steam or warm the milk, then pour it over the syrup; omit the ice. Top with the espresso and a drizzle of caramel sauce.*

Homemade Vanilla Syrup

MAKES 8 OUNCES

1 cup **granulated sugar**

8 ounces **water**

¼ teaspoon **kosher salt**

½ tablespoon **vanilla extract**

1. In a small saucepan, combine the sugar, water, and salt and bring to a simmer over medium-low heat. Simmer for 10 minutes.

2. Remove the syrup from the heat and stir in the vanilla extract. Use right away, or let cool completely, transfer to an airtight container, and store in the fridge for up to 3 weeks.

BANANA CREAM PIE BREVE

I am a sucker for a slice of banana cream pie. The decadent custard filling, the whipped topping, and the sliced banana, ooh, baby. This cozy breve replicates many of the classic banana cream pie flavors in a rich, smooth coffee form. The half-and-half makes the drink extra velvety and indulgent, and the ripe banana gives it that perfect sweet real banana flavor, no artificial tastes here. I love topping it with a generous scoop of Cool Whip for a touch more sweetness and some pie nostalgia, or you could add a sprinkle of ground cinnamon for some spice. **SERVES 1**

½ ripe **banana**

4 to 6 ounces **half-and-half**

1 tablespoon **maple syrup**

¼ teaspoon **vanilla extract**

⅛ teaspoon **kosher salt**

2 shots **espresso** (about 2 ounces), to brew

Cool Whip (optional)

1. In a blender, combine the banana, half-and-half, maple syrup, vanilla extract, and salt and blend until smooth.

2. Using your preferred method (see page 56), brew the espresso shots into a 12-ounce mug.

3. Steam the banana mixture using your preferred method (see page 64), then pour it over the espresso.

4. Top with a spoonful of Cool Whip, if using, and enjoy.

Make It Iced: *Follow step 1, then, using a 16-ounce glass, brew the espresso and add the banana cream mixture and ice cubes, followed by Cool Whip, if using.*

Make It Dairy-Free: *I prefer using a dairy-free half-and-half for this recipe (and all the other breve recipes in this book). The Nutpods brand is my favorite option—it's rich and creamy, like regular half-and-half, but without the dairy.*

HAZELNUT OAT MILK SHAKEN ESPRESSO

A shaken espresso is made by shaking together espresso, ice, and sweetener or flavoring until the mixture is chilled and foamy. Shaking aerates the drink, giving it a more frothy texture and fully chilling it. At Starbucks, the shaken espressos are made with an extra shot of espresso, so they also have a stronger coffee taste than a traditional latte. Starbucks' Hazelnut Oatmilk Shaken Espresso isn't usually garnished with ground cinnamon, but I think it elevates the flavor so perfectly that you have to try it. **SERVES 1**

1 to 2 tablespoons **Homemade Hazelnut Syrup** (recipe follows), or store-bought

3 shots **espresso** (about 3 ounces), to brew

Ice cubes

8 ounces **oat milk**

Ground cinnamon for garnish (optional)

1. Using your preferred method (see page 56), brew the espresso shots, then add them to a cocktail shaker or 16-ounce Mason jar.

2. Add the hazelnut syrup to taste and ice.

3. Cover the shaker or jar with the lid and shake until it is cold to the touch and the espresso mixture is chilled and foamy.

4. Pour the espresso mixture into a 16-ounce glass and top with the oat milk and cinnamon, if using, and enjoy.

Make It Hot: *Add the hazelnut syrup to a 12-ounce mug, then brew the espresso shots directly over the syrup; omit the ice. Steam or warm the oat milk and add it to the espresso mixture, and garnish with ground cinnamon, if using.*

Homemade Hazelnut Syrup

MAKES 10 OUNCES

1 cup **hazelnuts**, roasted and salted (see Note)

1 cup **granulated sugar**

8 ounces **water**

½ teaspoon **kosher salt**

¼ teaspoon **almond extract**

1. In a small saucepan, combine the hazelnuts, sugar, water, and salt. Stir to dissolve the sugar, then bring to a boil over high heat.

2. Reduce the heat to low and simmer for 10 minutes.

3. Remove from the heat and pour the syrup through a strainer into a Mason jar or heatproof container. Reserve the hazelnuts, if desired (see Note).

4. Stir in the almond extract.

5. Use the syrup right away, or let it cool completely, cover, and store in the fridge for up to 3 weeks.

Note: To roast and salt the hazelnuts: Heat a skillet over medium heat. Toast the hazelnuts in a single layer, stirring until fragrant and golden (5 to 10 minutes). Transfer the roasted hazelnuts to a towel and rub together to remove the skins. While warm, toss with a generous pinch of salt.

Note: Spread the reserved hazelnuts in a single layer on a parchment paper–lined baking sheet and bake in a 350°F oven for 10 to 15 minutes, stirring halfway through, until lightly browned and toasted. Let cool before enjoying. Store in an airtight container at room temperature for up to 1 week.

LEMON-ROSEMARY ESPRESSO TONIC

If you're looking for a refreshing switch up to your usual espresso routine, this espresso tonic with fresh lemon juice and a hint of rosemary just might be it. Bright lemon, bubbly tonic water, and the herbal sweetness of homemade rosemary syrup come together for a drink that's crisp, complex, and unexpectedly delightful. Pouring the espresso over the top results in a beautiful layered look and a bold kick of flavor. And while the rosemary syrup takes a little extra effort, it's so worth it—and you'll want to use it in everything from iced lattes to sparkling mocktails. With its citrusy, herbal notes and eye-catching presentation, this is the kind of drink that feels fancy but is deceptively simple to make. **SERVES 1**

Ice cubes

8 ounces **tonic water**

½ tablespoon **lemon juice**

1 to 2 tablespoons **Homemade Rosemary Syrup** (recipe follows), or store-bought

2 shots **espresso** (about 2 ounces), to brew

Sprig of **rosemary** for garnish (optional)

Lemon twist for garnish (optional)

1. Fill a 16-ounce glass with ice cubes, then add the tonic water, lemon juice, and rosemary syrup and stir to combine.

2. Using your preferred method (see page 56), brew the espresso shots into an 8-ounce mug.

3. Carefully pour the hot espresso over the top of the tonic water mixture.

4. Garnish with the sprig of rosemary and lemon twist, if using, and enjoy.

Homemade Rosemary Syrup

MAKES 10 OUNCES

1 cup **granulated sugar**

8 ounces **water**

4 sprigs **rosemary**

¼ teaspoon **kosher salt**

1. In a small saucepan, combine the sugar, water, rosemary, and salt. Stir to combine and bring to a boil over high heat.

2. Reduce the heat and simmer for 10 minutes.

3. Remove the saucepan from the heat and pour the syrup through a strainer or cheesecloth into a Mason jar or heatproof container. Discard the rosemary leaves.

4. Use the syrup right away, or let it cool completely, cover, and store in the fridge for up to 3 weeks.

BROWN SUGAR OAT MILK SHAKEN ESPRESSO

Arguably one of the best drinks on the Starbucks menu, the Brown Sugar Oatmilk Shaken Espresso was the very first "Copy Kat" recipe I tried to re-create at home. When my husband, Gabriel, and I got our fancy Breville espresso machine, this was the drink we were most excited to master. This drink sparked my passion for making coffee at home and ultimately launched my journey as a coffee content creator. **SERVES 1**

3 shots **espresso** (about 3 ounces), to brew

1 to 2 tablespoons **Homemade Brown Sugar Syrup** (recipe follows), or store-bought

1 teaspoon **ground cinnamon**

Ice cubes

6 to 8 ounces **oat milk**

1. Using your preferred method (see page 56), brew the espresso shots, then add them to a cocktail shaker or 16-ounce Mason jar.

2. Add the brown sugar syrup to taste, the cinnamon, and ice. Cover the shaker or jar with the lid and shake until it is cold to the touch and the espresso mixture is chilled and foamy.

3. Pour the espresso mixture, with ice, into a 16-ounce glass and top with the oat milk. Enjoy.

Make It Hot: *In a 12-ounce mug, combine the brown sugar syrup, cinnamon, and espresso; omit the ice. Steam or warm the oat milk and add it to the espresso mixture.*

Homemade Brown Sugar Syrup

MAKES 10 OUNCES

1 cup packed **dark brown sugar**

8 ounces **water**

½ teaspoon **kosher salt**

½ teaspoon **vanilla extract**

1. In a small saucepan, combine the dark brown sugar, water, and salt and stir well. Bring the mixture to a boil over high heat.

2. Reduce the heat to low and simmer for 10 minutes.

3. Remove from the heat and stir in the vanilla extract.

4. Use the syrup right away, or let it cool completely, transfer to an airtight container, and store in the fridge for up to 3 weeks.

ICED ORANGE CREAMSICLE AMERICANO

I always feel so fancy when drinking an Americano. It tastes and feels like an elevated coffee, and there's something about how light and refreshing it is that makes you want to make two or three (or four!) more. Americanos are made by combining espresso with water for all the fabulous taste and characteristics of espresso, but in a larger, milder-tasting cup than just straight espresso shots. This recipe combines sunny orange juice with a splash of vanilla and heavy cream for a beautifully balanced and complex iced beverage. **SERVES 1**

2 ounces **orange juice**

1 ounce **heavy cream** or **coconut cream**

½ teaspoon **vanilla extract**

Ice cubes

4 ounces **water**

2 shots **espresso** (about 2 ounces), to brew

1. In a 16-ounce Mason jar, combine the orange juice, heavy cream, and vanilla extract. Cover with the lid and shake until fully combined.

2. Fill a 16-ounce glass with ice and add the water. Pour the shaken orange cream mixture into the glass.

3. Using your preferred method (see page 56), brew the espresso shots, then pour over the orange cream mixture.

4. Gently stir to combine and enjoy.

Make It Hot: *Steam the water with the orange juice, heavy cream, and vanilla extract, then add to a 12-ounce mug. Omit the ice and top with the espresso shots.*

SALTED VANILLA AMERICANO

I do love a classic vanilla latte, but this Salted Vanilla Americano is a lighter, more intriguing take on that. It's smooth and comforting, with just enough of a salty twist to enhance the vanilla flavor in the best way. If you're still drinking plain brewed coffee every morning, I challenge you to switch things up with this simple yet elevated drink. **SERVES 1**

1 to 2 tablespoons **Homemade Vanilla Syrup** (page 146), or store-bought

Pinch of **kosher salt**

6 ounces **hot water**

2 shots **espresso** (about 2 ounces), to brew

1 ounce **heavy cream** or **milk** (optional)

1. In an 8-ounce mug, combine the vanilla syrup to taste and the salt.

2. Using your preferred method (see page 56), brew the espresso shots directly over the vanilla syrup.

3. Pour the hot water into a 12-ounce mug. Slowly pour the vanilla espresso mixture over the top.

4. Stir in the heavy cream or milk, if using, and enjoy.

Make It Iced: *Using a 16-ounce glass, follow steps 1 and 2, then add cold water and ice, followed by the heavy cream or milk, if using.*

SPARKLING PEACH ESPRESSO TONIC

I've been noticing that more and more coffee shops are including espresso tonics on their menus. At their simplest, these are iced beverages made using espresso and tonic water, often with a flavoring or sweetener. It's a refreshing, sweet, bubbly alternative to a traditional Americano, and it's great if you're looking for a fun mocktail-esque beverage that also feels very fancy and adult. Feel free to swap the tonic water for sparkling water or soda water for less sugar or use plain water for a Peach Americano. **SERVES 1**

Ice cubes

4 ounces **tonic water**

2 ounces **peach juice** or **peach nectar**

2 shots **espresso** (about 2 ounces), to brew

Sprig of **mint** for garnish (optional)

1. Fill a 16-ounce glass with ice, then add the tonic water and peach juice.

2. Using your preferred method (see page 56), brew the espresso shots into an 8-ounce mug.

3. Pour the espresso shots over the tonic mixture.

4. Stir gently to combine, and then garnish with the sprig of mint, if using, and enjoy.

COLD BREWS

& ICED COFFEES

CAMPFIRE COLD BREW

I may be dating myself here, but I grew up watching *The Sandlot*. It was a staple in our house, and quotes from the movie were part of our everyday vocabulary. If you don't know the movie, it's a 1993 classic with an iconic s'mores scene. So, this felt like the perfect excuse to give this nostalgic combo of chocolate and marshmallow a little love. First, you line the inside of the cup with Marshmallow Fluff. Then you pour in the cold brew. When the cocoa powder hits the top? You scarf. It's a simple, ridiculously delicious drink that'll have you saying, "You're killing me, Smalls," in the best way. **SERVES 1**

Marshmallow Fluff

Ice cubes

10 to 12 ounces **unsweetened cold brew**, homemade (page 58) or store-bought

2 ounces **chocolate milk**

Cocoa powder for garnish

1. Use the back of a spoon to spread a thin layer of Marshmallow Fluff all around the inside of a 20-ounce glass.

2. Add ice, the cold brew, and chocolate milk to the glass. Stir to combine, top with a sprinkle of cocoa powder, and enjoy.

DIY Chocolate Milk: *Make your own chocolate milk by combining 1 to 2 tablespoons chocolate sauce, homemade (page 78) or store-bought, and your choice of milk. Stir until fully combined.*

COCONUT CREAM COLD BREW

This Coconut Cream Cold Brew is like a slice of coconut cream pie in iced coffee form—sweet, bold, and refreshingly simple. The rich coconut cream creates a silky cold foam that pairs beautifully with the smooth bitterness of cold brew, while a touch of maple syrup adds just the right amount of sweetness. It's a quick and easy way to treat yourself, especially on warm days when you want something indulgent but still light. Topped with toasted coconut flakes, this drink delivers all the flavor of a dessert without having to turn on the oven. **SERVES 1**

10 to 12 ounces **unsweetened cold brew**, homemade (page 58) or store-bought

Ice cubes

2 tablespoons **maple syrup**

2 ounces canned **coconut whipping cream**, chilled

Toasted coconut flakes for garnish (optional)

1. Fill a 20-ounce glass with ice, then add the cold brew and 1 tablespoon of the maple syrup. Stir to combine.

2. In a small glass, combine the remaining 1 tablespoon of maple syrup and the coconut whipping cream and froth with a handheld milk frother until thick, 15 to 30 seconds.

3. Slowly pour the coconut cream cold foam over the cold brew, top with a sprinkle of toasted coconut flakes, if using, and enjoy.

PISTACHIO DREAM COLD BREW

Does anyone else plan their next morning's coffee while lying in bed the night before, or is that just me? This pistachio-flavored cold brew was one of those late-night ideas that turned out even better than I'd imagined. With buttery, nutty notes from pistachio and the smooth sweetness of white chocolate, you get this refreshingly dreamy cold brew that's just indulgent enough to feel like a little treat. Trust me, you'll be daydreaming about it in no time. **SERVES 1**

1 to 2 tablespoons **pistachio butter** or **pistachio cream**

1 to 2 tablespoons **Homemade White Chocolate Sauce** (page 81), or store-bought

1 ounce **half-and-half** or **heavy cream**

10 to 12 ounces **unsweetened cold brew**, homemade (page 58) or store-bought

Ice cubes

1. In a blender, combine the pistachio butter, white chocolate sauce, half-and-half or heavy cream, and cold brew and blend until smooth.

2. Fill a 20-ounce glass with ice, then add the pistachio cold brew mixture. Stir to combine and enjoy.

HONEYCOMB COLD BREW

I love this recipe because it proves how simple and delicious at-home coffee can be. These are all ingredients you can get at the grocery store—lavender extract is often found in the supplements aisle. You can use a store-bought cold brew like SToK for convenience, or make your own (see page 58). Adjust the sweetness level and lavender to your taste, if necessary, and you get a lovely, honeyed floral coffee that would be $7 at a coffee shop but costs less than $2 to make at home. **SERVES 1**

1 to 2 tablespoons **honey**

⅛ teaspoon **lavender extract**, or to taste

2 ounces **oat milk**

Ice cubes

10 to 12 ounces **unsweetened cold brew**, homemade (page 58) or store-bought

1. In a 20-ounce glass, combine the honey to taste, the lavender extract, and oat milk. Froth with a handheld milk frother until the honey is dissolved and the mixture is thoroughly combined.

2. Add ice and the cold brew, stir to combine, and enjoy.

PUMPKIN CREAM COLD BREW

When Starbucks first introduced their Pumpkin Cream Cold Brew, it quickly became a daily ritual for my husband and me—we were hooked. But when the following fall rolled around, something had changed. The drink tasted different, and the signature pumpkin spice topping was missing. Disappointed but determined, I set out to re-create the original magic at home. The result? A creamy, spiced cold brew with a pillowy cold foam that tastes like pumpkin, balanced with hints of vanilla and sweetened condensed milk. My husband loved it so much, he started requesting it daily, and years later, it's still his go-to. With this recipe, you don't have to wait for fall. You can enjoy a better-than-the-original Pumpkin Cream Cold Brew any time of year, made fresh in your own kitchen. **SERVES 1**

Ice cubes

½ to 1 tablespoon **Homemade Vanilla Syrup** (page 146), or store-bought

10 to 12 ounces **unsweetened cold brew**, homemade (page 58) or store-bought

PUMPKIN CREAM COLD FOAM

1 tablespoon canned **pumpkin puree**

½ tablespoon **Homemade Vanilla Syrup** (page 146), or store-bought

Pinch of **kosher salt**

½ tablespoon **sweetened condensed milk**

2 tablespoons **heavy cream**

2 tablespoons **2% milk**

Pumpkin pie spice for garnish

1. In a 20-ounce glass, combine ice, the vanilla syrup to taste, and the cold brew. Stir to blend, then set aside.

2. Make the cold foam: In an 8-ounce glass, combine the pumpkin puree, vanilla syrup, salt, condensed milk, cream, and 2% milk and froth with a handheld milk frother until thick and creamy, about 30 seconds.

3. Gently pour the foam over the cold brew, then sprinkle with pumpkin pie spice and enjoy.

BUTTER PECAN COLD BREW

My grandma's absolute favorite ice cream in the world was butter pecan. Anytime I'd ask Wella (Abuela is grandmother in Spanish, but I called her Wella for short) what kind of ice cream we should get, the answer was always butter pecan. She loved getting a scoop of Thrifty's ice cream from Water & Ice, and she'd always say "Kay [she always said Kay instead of Kat] let's go to Thrifty's for some butter pecan." She passed away in April 2023 and I miss her every single day. This one's for you, Wella.

SERVES 1

Ice cubes

1 to 2 tablespoons **Homemade Butter Pecan Syrup** (page 123), or store-bought

10 to 12 ounces **unsweetened cold brew**, homemade (page 58) or store-bought

1 to 3 tablespoons **heavy cream** or **half-and-half**

1. Fill a 20-ounce glass with ice, then add the butter pecan syrup to taste, the cold brew, and heavy cream or half-and-half.

2. Stir to combine and enjoy.

MAPLE–BROWN SUGAR COLD BREW

You know the maple-and-brown sugar oatmeal packets we used to devour as kids? (Please tell me I wasn't the only one obsessed with them.) This cold brew is essentially those same cozy flavors—sweet maple, warm brown sugar—but better, because it also has coffee. And instead of waiting on the microwave, you just toss everything into a blender, blend it up, and pour it over ice. It's creamy, nostalgic, and the perfect grown-up way to start your morning. **SERVES 1**

½ to 1 tablespoon **maple syrup**

½ to 1 tablespoon **dark brown sugar**

1 teaspoon **ground cinnamon**, plus more for garnish

¼ teaspoon **vanilla extract**

Pinch of **kosher salt**

2 tablespoons **heavy cream** or **half-and-half**

10 to 12 ounces **unsweetened cold brew**, homemade (page 58) or store-bought

Ice cubes

1. In a blender, combine the maple syrup and brown sugar to taste, the cinnamon, vanilla, salt, heavy cream or half-and-half, and cold brew and blend until smooth and creamy.

2. Fill a 20-ounce glass with ice, then add the cold brew.

3. Top with a sprinkle of cinnamon and enjoy.

HAZELNUT–IRISH CREAM COLD BREW

This cold brew is like a little sip of the luck of the Irish—smooth, sweet, and delightfully indulgent. The drink layers bold, cold brew with a swirl of homemade Irish Cream Syrup and is topped with a nutty hazelnut cold foam. A dusting of cocoa powder finishes it off, for that extra hint of magic. It's a festive treat for St. Patrick's Day—or any day you're craving a bit of coffeehouse charm with a touch of luck on top. **SERVES 1**

Ice cubes

1 to 2 tablespoons **Homemade Irish Cream Syrup** (page 120), or store-bought

10 to 12 ounces **unsweetened cold brew**, homemade (page 58) or store-bought

HAZELNUT COLD FOAM

1 tablespoon **Homemade Hazelnut Syrup** (page 152), or store-bought

2 tablespoons **2% milk**

3 tablespoons **heavy cream**

Cocoa powder for garnish

1. Fill a 20-ounce glass with ice and add the Irish cream syrup and cold brew. Stir to combine, and set aside.

2. Make the cold foam: In an 8-ounce glass, combine the hazelnut syrup, 2% milk, and heavy cream and froth with a handheld milk frother until thick and creamy, 15 to 30 seconds.

3. Gently pour the foam over the cold brew, sprinkle cocoa powder on top, and enjoy.

SALTED CARAMEL SWIRL ICED COFFEE

When it comes to iced coffee, I'm referring to hot brewed coffee that is poured over ice. This is different from an iced latte, where you'd need to brew espresso for the drink, and it's different from cold brew where you steep coffee grounds in room temperature water overnight. For iced coffee, you use your favorite brewing method—French press, coffee pot, Keurig, pour-over, AeroPress, Moka pot, etc. (see page 50)—to brew hot coffee, and then you add ice, along with your favorite mix-ins: in this case, a glorious drizzle of salted caramel sauce and half-and-half for a perfectly "not too sweet" iced coffee.

SERVES 1

1 to 2 tablespoons **Homemade Salted Caramel Sauce** (page 84), or store-bought, plus more for drizzling

8 to 10 ounces **brewed coffee** (see page 51)

1 to 2 ounces **half-and-half** or **heavy cream**

Ice cubes

1. Add the salted caramel sauce to taste to a 12-ounce mug.

2. Using your preferred method (see page 51), brew the coffee directly over the caramel sauce.

3. Stir the coffee or froth with a handheld milk frother until the caramel sauce is fully dissolved, then stir in the half-and-half.

4. Fill a 24-ounce glass with ice and pour the hot coffee over ice. Stir until the glass feels cold to the touch.

5. Drizzle a generous amount of salted caramel sauce over the top of the coffee, and enjoy.

CHOCOBANANA ICED COFFEE

Banana and chocolate are one of those classic flavor pairings that just work—sweet, creamy, and a little indulgent, without being over the top. This iced coffee brings those flavors together in the dreamiest way: the banana adds sweetness and body, while the chocolate sauce gives it a rich, mocha-like vibe. It's smooth and slightly frothy, and it tastes as if a dessert and a coffee had a beautiful baby. I love blending it all up for a café-style treat that feels just a little extra. Perfect for sipping slowly while pretending you're not procrastinating over your to-do list.

SERVES 1

8 to 10 ounces **brewed coffee** (see page 51), hot or chilled

½ ripe **banana**

1 to 2 ounces **heavy cream** or **half-and-half**

1 to 2 tablespoons **Homemade Chocolate Sauce** (page 78), or store-bought

Ice cubes

1. In a blender, combine the brewed coffee, banana, heavy cream, and chocolate sauce and blend until smooth and creamy.

2. Fill a 24-ounce glass with ice and add the banana coffee mixture.

3. Stir until the glass feels cold to the touch and enjoy.

DALGONA ICED COFFEE

Dalgona coffee had its big moment during the early days of the pandemic, when many of us found ourselves spending a lot more time at home and getting creative with our coffee routines. Made by whisking together instant coffee, sugar, and hot water until transformed into a light, mousse-like whip, Dalgona is equal parts fun and delicious and tastes like a creamy coffee dessert in a cup. While the trend may have come and gone, I think it's worth revisiting. You can even customize it by swapping the sugar for a flavored sweetener like my Homemade Salted Caramel Sauce (page 84) or Homemade Hazelnut Syrup (page 152) for your own version of the classic.

SERVES 1

1 tablespoon **instant coffee**

1 tablespoon **granulated sugar** (or other sweetener of choice)

1 tablespoon **hot water**

Ice cubes

8 ounces **milk** of choice

1. In a 12-ounce mug, combine the instant coffee, sugar, and hot water and froth with a handheld milk frother until thick and fluffy, about 30 seconds.

2. Fill a 16-ounce glass with ice and add the milk.

3. Top with the fluffy coffee mixture, stir gently to combine, and enjoy.

VIETNAMESE ICED COFFEE

My husband, Gabriel, and I have a favorite local Vietnamese restaurant (shoutout to Viet Shack!), and every time we go, without fail, Gabriel orders a Vietnamese iced coffee. Even if it's 7 p.m. and we're sitting down for dinner, he's sipping on his iced coffee. Vietnamese coffee is known for its bold, intense flavor, thanks to dark-roast Robusta coffee (often brewed with a phin filter), balanced by the creamy sweetness of condensed milk. The result? A strong, smooth, and incredibly flavorful drink that's just the right mix of rich and refreshing. It's coffee that gives you a delicious jolt—and keeps you coming back for more.

SERVES 1

1 to 3 tablespoons **sweetened condensed milk**

8 to 10 ounces **brewed coffee**

Ice cubes

1. In a 12-ounce mug, combine the condensed milk to taste and the hot coffee. Stir together until thoroughly combined.

2. Fill a 24-ounce glass with ice and add the hot coffee mixture.

3. Stir until the glass feels cold to the touch and enjoy.

Vietnamese Coffee Brewing Method: *Traditionally Vietnamese coffee is made using a phin filter (see page 53), but you can use any brewing method you prefer (see page 50).*

Best coffees to use with a phin filter: *Café du Monde, Trung Nguyen Coffee, Copper Cow Coffee Vietnamese Coffee*

CINNAMON CHURRO ICED COFFEE

We all want a churro every single day, correct? Well, good news, because you can now get cinnamon sugar churro goodness anytime, anywhere, no need for dough or oil or frying. Here it is in coffee form, which is really a dream come true. Get fancy with it and add a drizzle of Homemade Chocolate Sauce (page 78) and/or Homemade Salted Caramel Sauce (page 84), then close your eyes, take a sip, and imagine you're at Disneyland, riding "It's a Small World," churro in hand. **SERVES 1**

1 to 2 tablespoons **sweetened condensed milk**

1 teaspoon **ground cinnamon**

1 to 2 ounces **heavy cream** or **milk** of choice

8 to 10 ounces **brewed coffee** (see page 51), hot or chilled

Ice cubes

1. In a 12-ounce mug, combine the condensed milk to taste, the cinnamon, heavy cream to taste, and the coffee, then froth together with a handheld milk frother until frothy.

2. Fill a 24-ounce glass with ice and add the coffee mixture. Stir until the glass feels cold to the touch and enjoy.

THAI ICED COFFEE

I love Thai iced coffee! It's similar to Vietnamese iced coffee in its rich, sweet flavor from condensed milk, but with its own unique twist. Instead of using Robusta beans and a phin filter like the Vietnamese version, Thai iced coffee is traditionally made with Arabica beans brewed in a cafetière (or a French press). In addition to the condensed milk, it often has a splash of evaporated milk or cream, and it is infused with warm spices like cardamom. This version keeps it simple but flavorful, with just a touch of almond extract and ground cardamom to provide those classic Thai notes. Poured over ice and finished with a swirl of cream, it's bold, sweet, and perfectly refreshing.

SERVES 1

1 to 2 tablespoons **sweetened condensed milk**

⅛ teaspoon **almond extract**

⅛ teaspoon **ground cardamom**

8 to 10 ounces **brewed coffee** (see page 51)

Ice cubes

1 to 2 tablespoons **heavy cream**

1. In a 12-ounce mug, combine the sweetened condensed milk to taste, the almond extract, and cardamom.

2. Using your preferred method (see page 50), brew the coffee directly over the condensed milk mixture, then stir to combine.

3. Fill a 24-ounce glass with ice and add the coffee mixture.

4. Slowly pour the heavy cream to taste over the top of the coffee and stir until the glass feels cold to the touch. Enjoy.

HORCHATA ICED COFFEE

Horchata is a beloved drink in Hispanic culture—creamy, sweet, and spiced with cinnamon. Traditionally made by soaking rice and blending it with milk, cinnamon, vanilla, and sweetened condensed milk or sugar, it's a staple at many Mexican restaurants and taco stands. This recipe brings the essence of horchata into the world of coffee by combining its key ingredients with freshly brewed coffee for a deliciously sweet and spiced drink that nods to Mexican tradition. **SERVES 1**

1 to 2 tablespoons **sweetened condensed milk**

1 teaspoon **ground cinnamon**, plus more for garnish

3 ounces **rice milk**

¼ teaspoon **vanilla extract**

Pinch of **kosher salt**

8 to 10 ounces **brewed coffee** (see page 51), hot or chilled

Ice cubes

1. In a blender, combine the sweetened condensed milk to taste, the cinnamon, rice milk, vanilla, salt, and coffee and blend until smooth and creamy.

2. Fill a 24-ounce glass with ice and add the coffee mixture. Stir until the glass feels cold to the touch, then top with a sprinkle of ground cinnamon and enjoy.

GREEK FRAPPE ICED COFFEE

If you enjoyed the whipped coffee craze (hello Dalgona, page 186), you'll love the Greek Frappe! It's a simpler, more classic version that's been around much longer. Made with instant coffee, sugar, and cold water, this frothy iced drink skips the milk base of Dalgona and leans more toward an iced Americano in style. It's light and refreshing, especially with a splash of milk or cream for extra richness. Perfect for hot days or whenever you want a no-fuss coffee with a little foam on top, this recipe proves that instant coffee can absolutely hold its own. **SERVES 1**

2 teaspoons **instant coffee powder**

2 teaspoons **granulated sugar** (or other sweetener of choice)

6 ounces **cold water**

Ice cubes

1 ounce **milk** of choice or **heavy cream** (optional)

1. In a 24-ounce glass, combine the instant coffee, sugar, and cold water and froth with a handheld milk frother until frothy, about 30 seconds.

2. Add ice to the glass, then add the milk, if using, gently stir to combine, and enjoy.

BLENDED

& BONUS

VANILLA BEAN FRAPPE

When you're craving something creamy, dreamy, and totally coffee-free, this is the blended drink to make. The vanilla bean and maple syrup combo gives serious *vanilla bean ice cream in a cup* vibes, but it's way more fun to sip through a straw. The xanthan gum powder (find this online or in the grocery store baking aisle) gives the frappe a smoothy creamy texture, but be sure to only use ⅛ teaspoon to keep it from getting gummy. I know this classic frappe is one you'll be making on repeat. Oh, and trust me on this, drizzle some Homemade Salted Caramel Sauce (page 84) around the inside of your glass before pouring in the frappe. It'll taste approximately five thousand times better. **SERVES 1**

8 ounces **milk** of choice

1 to 2 tablespoons **maple syrup**

½ tablespoon **vanilla bean paste**

⅛ teaspoon **kosher salt**

⅛ teaspoon **xanthan gum** (optional)

1¼ cups **ice cubes**

Whipped cream (optional)

1. In a blender, combine the milk, maple syrup to taste, the vanilla paste, salt, xanthan gum, if using, and ice and blend until smooth and creamy.

2. Pour the frappe into a 20-ounce glass, top with whipped cream, if using, and enjoy.

Make It a Coffee Frappe: *Add 2 teaspoons instant coffee powder or 1 to 2 shots of espresso to the blender for a caffeine boost.*

WHITE MOCHA FRAPPE

We all know and love the infamous white mocha (page 81), but have you tried it blended? It's a refreshingly elevated way to enjoy the classic white chocolate and espresso combo. But if you're looking for a bit more pizzazz, feel free to add peppermint syrup, lavender extract, or Homemade Chocolate Sauce (page 78). **SERVES 1**

8 ounces **milk** of choice

1 to 2 tablespoons **Homemade White Chocolate Sauce** (page 81), or store-bought

2 teaspoons **instant coffee powder**

⅛ teaspoon **xanthan gum** (optional)

1¼ cups **ice cubes**

Whipped cream (optional)

1. In a blender, combine the milk, white chocolate sauce, instant coffee, xanthan gum, if using, and ice, and blend until smooth and creamy.

2. Pour the frappe into a 20-ounce glass, top with whipped cream, if using, and enjoy.

Make It Caffeine-Free: *Skip the instant coffee to make this a plain crème frappe.*

PEPPERMINT MOCHA FRAPPE

This recipe is for people who love to drink iced coffee year-round, especially those who believe peppermint mocha season should never end. Blended with creamy milk, rich chocolate sauce, and a refreshing burst of peppermint, this frappe is just as delicious in the middle of July as it is in December. Skip the instant coffee for a plain crème version or use chocolate milk for an extra-chocolatey treat. **SERVES 1**

½ to 1 tablespoon **Homemade Peppermint Syrup** (page 97), or store-bought

½ to 1 tablespoon **Homemade Chocolate Sauce** (page 78), or store-bought

8 ounces **milk** of choice

⅛ teaspoon **xanthan gum** (optional)

2 teaspoons **instant coffee powder**

1¼ cups **ice cubes**

Whipped cream (optional)

Crushed candy canes and **chocolate shavings** for garnish (optional)

1. In a blender, combine the peppermint syrup and chocolate sauce to taste, the milk, xanthan gum, if using, the instant coffee, and ice and blend until smooth and creamy.

2. Pour the frappe into a 20-ounce glass, top with whipped cream, if desired, and sprinkle with crushed candy canes and chocolate shavings, if using, and enjoy.

Make it Caffeine-Free: *Skip the instant coffee to make this a plain crème frappe.*

Make It a Peppermint White Mocha Frappe: *Swap the chocolate sauce for Homemade White Chocolate Sauce (page 81).*

SALTED CARAMEL FRAPPE

This is one of the recipes I believe everyone should have in their arsenal of drinks they make. It's simple and sweet, creamy and bold, and it comes together in two minutes. I love using my Homemade Salted Caramel Sauce (page 84), but you could easily substitute a store-bought caramel sauce like Torani to make it even simpler. You add everything to a blender, blend until smooth, and then top with whipped cream, if desired, and more caramel sauce. It's a beginner-friendly recipe that is a perfect pick-me-up for whatever life is throwing at you that day. **SERVES 1**

8 ounces **milk** of choice

1 to 2 tablespoons **Homemade Salted Caramel Sauce** (page 84), or store-bought, plus more for topping

2 teaspoons **instant coffee powder**

⅛ teaspoon **xanthan gum** (optional)

1¼ cups **ice cubes**

Whipped cream (optional)

1. In a blender, combine the milk, caramel sauce, instant coffee, xanthan gum, if using, and ice, and blend until smooth and creamy.

2. Pour the frappe into a 20-ounce glass, top with whipped cream, if using, and a drizzle of caramel sauce, and enjoy.

Make It Caffeine-Free: *Skip the instant coffee to make this a plain crème frappe.*

COUNTRY APPLE PIE FRAPPE

If there's one thing you should trust me on, it's that you absolutely need this frappe in your life. It tastes like vanilla ice cream on top of a warm freshly baked apple pie. The Homemade Apple Pie Sauce is one of those sauces where if you start to taste it to see if it's good, you then look down to realize you've "tasted" your way through the entire pan. This one is well worth writing home to grandma about. I hope you love it as much as I do. **SERVES 1**

8 ounces **milk** of choice

2 tablespoons **Homemade Apple Pie Sauce** (recipe follows)

½ tablespoon **vanilla bean paste**

⅛ teaspoon **xanthan gum** (optional)

1¼ cups **ice cubes**

Whipped cream (optional)

Apple pie spice for garnish (optional)

1. In a blender, combine the milk, apple pie sauce, vanilla paste, xanthan gum, if using, and ice and blend until smooth and creamy.

2. Pour the frappe into a 20-ounce glass, top with whipped cream and a sprinkle of apple pie spice, if using, and enjoy.

Make It a Coffee Frappe: *Add 2 teaspoons instant coffee powder or 1 to 2 shots of espresso for a caffeine boost.*

Homemade Apple Pie Sauce

MAKES 8 OUNCES

4 cups peeled, cored, and diced **apples**

½ cup packed **light** or **dark brown sugar**

2 tablespoons **lemon juice**

2 tablespoons **cornstarch**

1 teaspoon **ground cinnamon**

1 teaspoon **ground nutmeg**

Pinch of **kosher salt**

1 cup **apple juice**

1. In a medium saucepan, combine the apples, sugar, lemon juice, cornstarch, cinnamon, nutmeg, and salt, stir well, and bring to a simmer over medium-low heat.

2. Add the apple juice and stir constantly until the mixture thickens, 3 to 5 minutes. Remove from the heat.

3. Pour the sauce through a strainer into a Mason jar or heatproof container. Reserve the apple pieces, if desired (see Note).

4. Use the sauce right away, or let it cool completely, cover, and store in the fridge for up to 3 weeks.

Note: Store the drained apples in an airtight container in the fridge for up to 1 week. Use as a topping for frappes, pancakes, French toast, waffles, oatmeal, yogurt, or ice cream.

STRAWBERRY SHAKER

This Strawberry Shaker is my copycat version of the infamous Starbucks Pink Drink made with strawberry-infused grape juice, coconut milk, and a hint of caffeine from the green coffee bean powder. I love making a big batch of the strawberry base and storing it in the fridge for easy grab-and-go pink drinks all week long. If you don't love the coconut milk version, use water in your cocktail shaker for a regular strawberry refresher or use lemonade for a lemonade version. **SERVES 10**

6 ounces **Homemade Strawberry Base** (recipe follows)

6 ounces **coconut milk**

A small handful of **freeze-dried strawberries**

Ice cubes

1 scoop (100 mg) **green coffee bean powder**, optional

1. In a cocktail shaker or 16-ounce Mason jar, combine the strawberry base, coconut milk, freeze-dried strawberries, ice, and coffee powder, if using.

2. Cover the shaker or jar and shake until the mixture is well combined and chilled. Pour the mixture into a 16-ounce glass, and enjoy.

Strawberry Base

MAKES 60 OUNCES

2½ cups fresh or frozen **strawberries**, washed and stems removed if fresh

64 ounces **white grape juice**

¼ teaspoon **kosher salt**

1 tablespoon **lemon juice**

1. In a large pot, combine the strawberries, grape juice, and salt and bring to a simmer over medium-low heat. Simmer for 15 minutes.

2. Pour the base through a strainer into a large pitcher or Mason jar (discard the strawberries), then stir in the lemon juice. Let cool completely, cover, and store in the fridge for up to 3 weeks.

SALTED MAPLE ESPRESSO MARTINI MOCKTAIL

This Martini Mocktail is for the party people skipping the booze, the expectant mamas (go decaf, if you like), or, truly, anyone who just wants a fun, fancy drink without the alcohol. It's creamy, sweet, and salty, with bold espresso, rich maple syrup, and a frothy finish that feels totally cocktail hour–worthy. Shake it up and serve it in a martini glass with a few coffee beans on top, and boom, you've got yourself the ultimate predinner pick-me-up or party sip: sophisticated, festive, and caffeine-fueled. **SERVES 1**

2 shots **espresso** (about 2 ounces), to brew

2 ounces **heavy cream**

1 ounce **maple syrup**

Pinch of **kosher salt**

Ice cubes

3 **coffee beans** for garnish

1. Using your preferred method (see page 56), brew the espresso shots into an 8-ounce mug.

2. Pour the espresso into a cocktail shaker and add the heavy cream, maple syrup, salt, and ice. Cover with the lid and shake the mixture for a full 60 seconds, until the shaker is very cold to the touch.

3. Strain the mocktail into a martini glass, carefully garnish with the coffee beans, and enjoy.

SALTED COOKIE BUTTER AFFOGATO

An affogato is a dessert made by pouring freshly brewed espresso over ice cream. If you've ever tried an affogato, you know just how heavenly they are—and so worth being up until 3 a.m. because you ordered one at a restaurant after dinner. And if you've never had one, this is your sign to try it. This one combines espresso and cookie butter, the best type of butter there is. You pour that mixture over two scoops of ice cream (or more, I'm not here to judge) and sprinkle with flaky sea salt for that perfect sweet-and-salty balance. Stop right now: You get the ice cream, I'll brew the espresso, and let's meet back here in five minutes. **SERVES 1**

1 tablespoon **cookie butter**

1 to 2 shots **espresso** (about 1 to 2 ounces), to brew

2 scoops **vanilla ice cream**

Pinch of **flaky sea salt**

1. Add the cookie butter to an 8-ounce mug.

2. Using your preferred method (see page 56), brew the espresso shots directly over the cookie butter. Gently stir until the cookie butter is fully melted and incorporated.

3. Add the ice cream to a serving bowl and pour the espresso mixture over it. Top with a sprinkle of flaky sea salt and enjoy.

CHOCOLATE-COVERED ORANGE AFFOGATO

This was another idea that came to me late at night while in bed, like the Pistachio Dream Cold Brew on page 170. I should've been sleeping, but instead I was thinking about how perfect oranges and chocolate are together and then thought, "Oh my gosh, that would make a great coffee combo!" I immediately added orange sherbert to my grocery list so I could whip it up the next day, and it did not disappoint. I recommend using a coffee with sweet chocolate flavor notes to make the espresso (see chart, page 41), but really, this is a recipe where it's right no matter how you do it. **SERVES 1**

1 to 2 shots **espresso** (1 to 2 ounces), to brew

2 scoops **orange sherbet**

1 to 2 tablespoons **Homemade Chocolate Sauce** (page 78), or store-bought

¼ teaspoon grated **orange zest**

1. Using your preferred method (see page 56), brew the espresso shots into an 8-ounce mug.

2. Add the sherbet to a serving bowl and pour the espresso over the top. Top with a drizzle of the chocolate sauce to taste and the orange zest and enjoy.

ACKNOWLEDGMENTS

To my sweet husband, Gabriel. Thank you for standing beside me through every chapter of this journey and for being the most enthusiastic taste tester I could ever dream of. You were the one who encouraged me to share my morning coffee videos in the first place, and you continue to remind me, gently and often, to approach life with joy and lightness. Thank you for patiently teaching me how to use the Breville (properly!), and for believing in this dream long before it became a manuscript. This book simply would not exist without your love, support, and unwavering confidence in me. I love you lots.

To my agent, Sydney Shiffman. Thank you for being the steady, thoughtful, and caring guide I didn't even know I needed. You've shown me again and again that no question is ever too small and no dream is ever out of reach. You've supported me through every step with such genuine kindness and clarity, and this book exists because you believed it in, and in me, from the very beginning. It is an honor to know you and a privilege to work with someone who brings such brilliance, empathy, and genuine excitement to everything you do. Your guidance and appreciation for great coffee shaped every part of this book, and I am endlessly grateful for your encouragement and expertise.

To my editor, Jennifer Sit. Thank you for believing so deeply in the at-home coffee concept and for guiding this book with such grace, wisdom, and eloquence. Your gift with words and your thoughtful approach made me feel supported at every turn, from our earliest conversations to the countless meetings, emails, and title-brainstorming sessions along the way. I cannot thank you enough for the care, patience, and encouragement you poured into this process. Working with you has been an absolute gift.

To Elaine Hennig. Your brilliant mind and extraordinary attention to detail have elevated this book in ways most readers will never realize, but I always will. You catch things that others overlook, and you approach every page with a dedication that reflects how much you care about creating something truly excellent. It has been a joy and a privilege to work alongside you. Thank you for the countless hours, the thoughtful notes, and the energy you invested in bringing this book to life.

To my incredibly talented photographer, Doaa Elkady; prop stylist, Julia Rose; and food stylist, Fatima Khami. Thank you for transforming each recipe into something breathtaking. Watching you work, each of you masterful in your craft, was one of the greatest honors of this entire experience. Your creativity, artistry, and commitment during our weeklong photoshoot exceeded anything I could have imagined. You brought these drinks to life with such beauty and intention, and I am in awe of the talent you poured into every detail. This book is richer because of you.

To my extraordinary illustrator, Elizabeth Hart. Your illustrations gave this book its soul. You somehow reached inside my imagination and drew what I didn't yet have words for. Thank you for lending your remarkable talent to these pages, and for making this book even more joyful, colorful, and alive than I dreamed.

To my designer and art director, Stephanie Huntwork. Thank you for turning my simple words and ideas into a book that feels truly magical. From the earliest moodboards to the final cover design, you brought a vision to life that I didn't even know how to articulate, but you understood it perfectly. Your talent, thoughtfulness, and creative intuition shine on every page. Thank you for transforming a dream into something tangible, beautiful, and so much better than I ever could have imagined.

To the entire Clarkson Potter team, including production editor, Serena Wang; production manager, Jessica Heim; publicist, Jina Stanfill; and marketer, Stephanie Davis. Thank you for helping turn this dream into a reality. Your talent, expertise, and countless behind-the-scenes efforts have guided this book from an idea into something truly beautiful. From the thoughtful conversations to the encouragement you offered at every stage, your dedication has meant more than I can express. You create books that make life more beautiful, delicious, and joyful, and I am deeply grateful that this one was shaped by your hands.

To my online community of "Barista Homies." Thank you for your endless encouragement, curiosity, and enthusiasm. Your questions, recipe requests, comments, and DMs have shaped and inspired this book from the very beginning. You have created a community rooted in joy, creativity, and connection, and I am endlessly grateful for each of you. My hope is that this book becomes well-worn and well-loved, filled with coffee stains, syrup drips, sticky notes, and fingerprints, as you craft your morning, afternoon, and anytime creations in the comfort of your own home.

And to my dad and mama. Thank you for being my greatest supporters for as long as I can remember. Every time my life has taken a new turn, you've met me with unwavering love, encouragement, and the steady belief that I could do anything I set my heart on. You've stood with me through the laughter and the tears, the victories and the challenges, and you've always reminded me to dream boldly and without hesitation. Thank you for letting me be your personal barista all these years, and for believing in me at every single step. This book carries pieces of both of you on every page.

INDEX

Clarkson Potter/Publishers
An imprint of the Crown Publishing Group
A division of Penguin Random House LLC
1745 Broadway
New York, NY 10019
clarksonpotter.com
penguinrandomhouse.com

Copyright © 2026 by Katerina Diaz

Photographs copyright © 2026 by Doaa Elkady
Penguin Random House values and supports copyright. Copyright fuels creativity, encourages diverse voices, promotes free speech, and creates a vibrant culture. Thank you for buying an authorized edition of this book and for complying with copyright laws by not reproducing, scanning, or distributing any part of it in any form without permission. You are supporting writers and allowing Penguin Random House to continue to publish books for every reader. Please note that no part of this book may be used or reproduced in any manner for the purpose of training artificial intelligence technologies or systems.

Clarkson Potter is a trademark and Potter with colophon is a registered trademark of Penguin Random House LLC.

Library of Congress Cataloging-in-Publication Data is available from the publisher.

ISBN 979-8-217-03510-6
Ebook ISBN 979-8-217-03511-3

Editor: Jennifer Sit | Editorial assistant: Elaine Hennig
Illustrator: Elizabeth Hart | Designer and art director: Stephanie Huntwork | Production designer: Christina Self
Production editor: Serena Wang
Production manager: Jessica Heim
Compositors: Merri Ann Morrell and Hannah Hunt
Food stylist: Fatima Khamise | Food stylist assistant: Melissa Moreland, Sage Foster, Simon Solberg
Prop stylist: Julia Rose | Prop stylist assistant: Andy Rapavy
Copyeditor: Judith Sutton
Proofreaders: Kate Bolen, Erica Rose, and Tess Rossi
Indexer: Eldes Tran
Publicist: Jina Stanfill
Marketer: Stephanie Davis

Manufactured in China

10 9 8 7 6 5 4 3 2 1

First Edition

The authorized representative in the EU for product safety and compliance is Penguin Random House Ireland, Morrison Chambers, 32 Nassau Street, Dublin D02 YH68, Ireland, https://eu-contact.penguin.ie.